Happiness, Economics and Public Policy

Happiness, Economics and Public Policy

HELEN JOHNS AND PAUL ORMEROD

WITH COMMENTARIES BY SAMUEL BRITTAN AND
MELANIE POWELL

The Institute of Economic Affairs

First published in Great Britain in 2007 by
The Institute of Economic Affairs
2 Lord North Street
Westminster
London SW1P 3LB
in association with Profile Books Ltd

The mission of the Institute of Economic Affairs is to improve public understanding of the fundamental institutions of a free society, by analysing and expounding the role of markets in solving economic and social problems.

A CIP catalogue record for this book is available from the British Library.

ISBN 978 0 255 36600 7

Many IEA publications are translated into languages other than English or are reprinted. Permission to translate or to reprint should be sought from the Director General at the address above.

Typeset in Stone by MacGuru Ltd
info@macguru.org.uk

Printed and bound in Great Britain by Hobbs the Printers

CONTENTS

THE AUTHORS

Helen Johns

Helen Johns is an economist specialising in the analysis of environmental policy. She has worked on a broad range of research projects for the UK government, the European Commission and the private sector in areas such as environmental trading schemes, non-market valuation, policy appraisal and assessing environmental liability. She started her career as a physicist, working with Paul Ormerod at Volterra Consulting before gaining her MSc in Environmental and Resource Economics at University College London under the late David Pearce.

Paul Ormerod

Paul Ormerod is an economist and director of Volterra Consulting. He is the author of three bestselling books, *The Death of Economics*, *Butterfly Economics* and *Why Most Things Fail*, the latter being *Business Week* US Business Book of the Year 2006. His main interests are complex systems and social networks, and he publishes in a wide range of journals, including *Physica A*, *Journal of Artificial Societies and Social Simulation* and *Diplomacy and Statecraft*.

FOREWORD

The authors of this monograph have done a brilliant job of 'unpicking' the tangled web of the economics of happiness.

It appears that 'happiness economics' is becoming influential in political circles. Politicians are running around promising to look after our gross national wellbeing instead of just looking after gross national product. But it is difficult to think of any subject within economics that is built on such insecure foundations. Furthermore, the translation of the economic ideas into political practice seems specifically oriented towards no purpose other than providing further excuses for interference in the lives of individuals by the political class.

First, let us consider the politics. It is clearly a misconception that governments through the ages have acted to try to maximise gross national product. For most of time, in most countries, gross national product has not been measurable in real time. Ironically, in the UK and the USA, it has only been during the post-war period that gross national product has been observable, yet policies have been followed that reduced growth below its potential by increasing regulation and taxes. The share of national income taken in taxes in nearly all developed countries is significantly above that which would allow economic welfare to be maximised. Politicians have never tried to maximise gross national product – and, if they have, they have not been very good at it. There is a straightforward cause of this phenomenon, of course. In general, politicians follow the courses of action that are most likely to get them elected. In the political market, vested interests and median voters are king. It may increase the happiness of politicians to tell us that they are going to maximise our wellbeing, but it is a task that is beyond their capacity.

The economics of happiness seems just as shaky as the politics. The proponents of the use of happiness measures argue that happiness has not risen with national income. People become happier, it is said, only when they are better off relative to others. We are therefore in a futile race to become happier, in effect, at the expense of others. On average, happiness does not increase with incomes.

As Helen Johns and Paul Ormerod show, aggregate measures of happiness over time are not, in fact, strongly correlated with any variable we would expect them to be correlated with – and this is unsurprising given the way happiness measures are constructed. Happiness measures are extremely insensitive indicators. Happiness, for example, is not correlated with improved life expectancy, government spending, disability, sexual inequality or unemployment. Relationships between happiness and crime appear, tentatively, to throw up a positive correlation! Policymakers have latched on to the apparent need to have a more even distribution of income to raise national happiness – something that many would regard as the legitimisation of envy, a vice that never brings happiness in the long term. Measured happiness has not, however, been affected by the widening of the disparity in incomes over the past 30 years or so, just as it has not been affected by the growth in average incomes.

There is no question that happiness data is being used selectively to justify preconceived beliefs about policy alternatives.

Helen Johns and Paul Ormerod are to be congratulated for their rigorous analysis, sifting through a highly complex subject area and bringing out the key points so effectively. One of those key points is that the happiness data does not tell us anything significant as far as economic relationships are concerned.

So if we accept the authors' conclusions, what are we to make of the use of gross national wellbeing in government policy? It appears clear from the evidence that happiness has much to do with personal values and dispositions. It also seems clear that we adjust our description of happiness according to our aspirations of what is attainable. If we live in a brick-built house, with food and clothing but few luxuries, we might feel happy, all other things being equal, in an era where most other people were just able to meet their basic needs. In a later generation, when many people own luxury goods, somebody who had these luxury goods might not feel any happier than a person on a modest living in an earlier generation. This is easy enough to explain. It is the natural human disposition to want to aspire to better things and to be a little restless and ambitious – to attain a little more than we have. As long as this improvement in living standards is not achieved at the expense of general welfare, why should we suppress the natural human desire for self-improvement just because it throws up some awkward questions for compilers of happiness statistics? In fact, we are simply taken back to the age-old political questions – what political and economic systems and policies are both in harmony with the natural human condition and lead to the highest levels of welfare? The desire by governments to plan our happiness will lead to a loss of liberty and a loss of welfare. Such efforts are as flawed as attempts by government to plan our economic activity.

Or perhaps we can just sum it all up in one phrase from

Hayek's *The Road to Serfdom* (Chapter V): 'The welfare and happiness of millions cannot be measured on a single scale of less and more.'

PHILIP BOOTH

Editorial and Programme Director,
Institute of Economic Affairs
Professor of Insurance and Risk Management,
Sir John Cass Business School, City University
June 2007

The views expressed in this monograph are, as in all IEA publications, those of the authors and not those of the Institute (which has no corporate view), its managing trustees, Academic Advisory Council members or senior staff.

SUMMARY

- Surveys on the levels of happiness reported by individuals
  have been carried out over a few decades in most Western
  countries. The recorded levels of happiness fluctuate from
  year to year. But in general there is no trend, either up or
  down, in this data. Over the same period, average material
  standards of living, measured by real gross national product
  (GNP) per head, have shown a very clear upward trend. So
  economic growth does not appear to improve the human lot.
  GNP per head has risen, but happiness has not.
- This finding has been widely publicised. It is used as the basis
  for wide-reaching policy recommendations. For example,
  taxation should be much more progressive, and hours of
  work should be restricted for everyone, because money does
  not make people feel better off. People need to be told how to
  be happier and, for their own good, taxed off their treadmills
  of overwork and consumption. Further, measures of national
  happiness should complement, or even replace, GNP as the
  main target of government policy.
- But there have been many other profound social and political
  trends over the past 60 years or so which might be expected
  to have affected happiness for good or ill. Public spending
  has risen substantially, longevity has increased markedly,
  and the degree of inequality between the sexes has fallen. But,

just as with GNP per head, the data on happiness over time shows no correlations with these changes. Even increases in recorded depression have not provoked shifts in recorded happiness. And the sharp rise in income inequality in the USA over the past 30 years has not reduced happiness.

- One could conclude from the lack of correlation over time between aggregate happiness and almost any other socio-economic variable of interest one of two things. Either that attempting to improve the human lot through economic or social policy is futile, or that happiness data over time is an extremely insensitive measure of welfare. The evidence points to the latter.

- A simple but important explanation is the way in which happiness is measured. People are asked to register their level of happiness on a scale that often has as few as three categories ('not happy', 'fairly happy' or 'very happy'). As a consequence, noticeable changes in average happiness can come about only through substantial numbers of people changing their categories.

- Much more fundamentally, this way of measuring happiness means there is an upper bound to the level of happiness that can ever be recorded. This creates very serious statistical problems when trying to correlate changes in a series that has an upper limit with one, such as GNP per head, that can in principle rise without limit.

- In addition, the more serious research on happiness has established that people adapt rapidly to changes in both their monetary and non-monetary circumstances. So the fact that reported happiness over time is not correlated with GNP per head or increased public spending, say, does not necessarily tell us very much at all. People become accustomed to the new, higher levels and would feel less happy if these were reduced to their previous levels.

- There is a body of research on happiness which is, from a scientific perspective, much more securely grounded. This is based upon the analysis, not of aggregate happiness data over time, but of so-called panel, or longitudinal, data, which tracks specific individuals over time. It shows that stable family life, being married, good health, having religious faith, feelings of living in a cohesive community where people can be trusted, and good governance contribute to happiness. Chronic pain, divorce and bereavement detract from happiness.

- The idea that GNP needs to be supplemented by a measure of 'gross national happiness' or wellbeing is similar to arguments for modifying GNP to account for environmental and other externalities. How such an indicator would actually produce better decisions is, however, rarely spelt out in detail. The use of even a sensitive happiness metric in public policy would be as vulnerable to anomalous and ethically questionable results and losses of information as any other numerical metric subject to crude maximisation.

- As an uncontroversial 'motherhood and apple pie' concept, happiness glosses over the very real trade-offs, creating winners and losers, that exist in any policy decision. Furthermore, there are areas where happiness arguments or evidence might produce or camouflage morally questionable outcomes. Not everything can be reduced to its effects on empirically observed happiness. Further, it will always be a political and moral call as to what happiness evidence is acceptable, throwing into doubt its usefulness as an objective measure.

- Democratic decision-making already takes into account many desirable outcomes other than economic growth. The dichotomy presented by many proponents of happiness research – that use of GNP implies a narrow, materialistic and self-centred view of welfare, while use of happiness indicators would imply a more holistic or ethical conception – is a false one.

- The logical conclusion of much happiness research – that individuals' own judgements about what is good for them can, indeed *should*, be overridden by experts who can 'prove' these judgements did not make them happier – is both undemocratic and unattractively paternalistic. While it is true that individual agents are not in general capable of following the maximising precepts of behaviour of economic theory, the idea that remote policymakers are able to do so in their stead should be treated with a great deal of scepticism.

FIGURES

Happiness, Economics and Public Policy

1 INTRODUCTION

The concept of happiness and its relationship to economics and politics is a very fashionable one. The 1990s saw an enormous increase in academic research into the concept, with no fewer than 4,351 articles being published by the year 2000 (Veenhoven, 2007). Since then, the flood has become a torrent.[1]

In the UK, policymakers are devoting increasing attention to happiness. There is, for example, a Whitehall Wellbeing Working Group and a committee on wellbeing research working in conjunction with the Department for Environment, Food and Rural Affairs. The Sustainable Development Commission is promoting research on 'how policies might change with an explicit wellbeing focus', and a cross-government wellbeing indicators group is developing a set of wellbeing measures for informing policy (to be unveiled this summer).

In one sense, the British government is finally catching up with the United States' Declaration of Independence of 1776, which regarded it as self-evident that the 'pursuit of happiness' was an 'inalienable right', comparable with life and liberty. In another, it is clearly debatable whether government should presume responsibility for individuals' emotional states.

---

1   Many of the key articles are cited in important papers in two of the world's top academic economic journals, e.g. Frey and Stutzer (2002a), Kahneman and Krueger (2006), Di Tella and MacCulloch (2006).

Whatever the driver, the notion of focusing government policy explicitly on engendering happiness is evidently touching a chord. This stems from a totally reasonable assessment that human welfare is derived from a great deal more than material goods. It is derived from the quality of one's personal relationships, from feelings of common cause and shared experience with others, from enjoyment of nature, and from good governance, among other things.

The question of what constitutes happiness has of course been a profound one in both philosophical and religious thinking for over two thousand years. It is not our purpose to enter into these intractable philosophical debates. We simply note that defining happiness is a question that has occupied some of the greatest minds in the Western world and yet it still remains open. So it is questionable whether it can easily be resolved by the application of simple policy recommendations.

It is important to say, however, that the concept of happiness is inherently subjective and is not necessarily connected to what most people would deem moral. For example, ethnic cleansing might well increase the happiness of those who do not like sharing their neighbourhood with people who are ethnically different from themselves, but it is not a course of action that could conceivably be deemed moral. We give specific examples of potential conflicts between morality and happiness at various points in the text.

The main focus of this monograph is on happiness research and public policy, where many strong claims are being made. For example, a key finding of happiness research is that in the developed world over the past 30 or 40 years happiness appears not to have increased despite the fact that real per capita incomes, and material living standards, have doubled. An explanation advanced for this in the happiness literature (Layard, 2005) is that it is essentially not the absolute level of income of a person or household which generates happiness, but the level of income relative to that of others. The implication drawn from this is that progressive taxation will reduce such relative disparities and will therefore increase overall happiness.

We take issue with this and with many other findings of happiness research. More particularly, we take issue with their interpretation. Our principal criticisms are that:

- Time-series of measured happiness show there has been little variation over the past 50 years. Yet happiness research itself suggests that many of the huge social and economic changes that have taken place should have made a difference to happiness. This indicates that happiness data over time is an extremely insensitive measure of welfare.
- Supposed relationships found between happiness and macroeconomic variables such as unemployment and inflation are far too unreliable and unstable to be of use in policymaking.
- The use of even a sensitive happiness metric in public policy would be as vulnerable to anomalous and ethically questionable results and losses of information as any other numerical metric, and more vulnerable to one-sided interpretation.
- The premise implicit in much happiness policy advocacy, that government policy is only concerned with maximising national income, is false.

Happiness research also has implications for economic theory and, in particular, the postulates on which individual behaviour is based in such theory. This work has a much more secure foundation, being supported by a wide range of work in experimental economics over the past 25 years. We begin in Chapter 2 with a short discussion of this aspect of happiness research.

We move on in Chapter 3 to discuss at considerably greater length some of the key findings in the happiness literature which are used in the current policy debate. In Chapter 4 we consider briefly the 'macroeconomic' policy claims made on the basis of happiness research. Chapter 5 discusses the concept of 'gross national happiness' in comparison with the more conventional, economic-based gross national product. Chapter 6 illustrates how happiness evidence might be used in a policy context, using the example of environmental protection; and the final chapter discusses the potential moral ambiguity of some happiness policy suggestions and offers conclusions.

As a final point in this introduction, we note that the terms 'happiness', 'wellbeing' and 'life satisfaction' are used interchangeably by many researchers, and will also be used interchangeably in this monograph. The term 'subjective wellbeing' refers to self-reported happiness. Wellbeing is frequently referred to in the literature as accounting for 'elements of life satisfaction which cannot be defined, explained or primarily influenced by economic growth' (SDRN, 2006).

2 HAPPINESS RESEARCH AND ECONOMIC THEORY

By far the most publicised finding of happiness research, noted above, is the lack of correlation over time within individual countries between reported happiness and real GDP per head. We discuss this at considerable length in Chapter 3 below. Two different results from the literature appear, however, to have important implications for economic theory.

Happiness is positively correlated with individual income within a given country in any given year: the rich generally report greater happiness than the poor at any given point in time. Second, the increase in happiness associated with income within the same country at a point in time appears to get smaller and smaller as income increases.

These two points seem to provide evidence consistent with a basic but essential postulate in standard economic theory, that of diminishing marginal utility. In other words, the additional benefits conferred by each extra unit of consumption of a service or a product, or by an extra unit of income, become smaller and smaller as the level of consumption or income rises. The opinion that happiness research confirms diminishing marginal utility is spreading within the happiness literature (for example, Frey and Stutzer, 2002a).

There are two technical points to be made here. First, what appears to have been established is a relationship between *reported* happiness and income. We do not, however, know the shape of the function that relates reported happiness to *actual* happiness. Andrew Oswald demonstrates that, as a result, we cannot reliably infer diminishing marginal utility from the happiness literature. His argument, although short, is mathematical and interested readers are referred to his article (Oswald, 2005).

The second point has been made recently by Richard East-erlin of the University of Southern California, in many ways the founding father of modern research on happiness. The lack of correlation between GDP and happiness has been established using data on reported happiness over time (that is, using 'time-series' data). The two findings that appear to establish diminishing marginal utility of income emerge from analysis of data at a point in time (that, is using 'cross-section data').

Easterlin's argument, which is empirical in contrast to the theoretical one of Oswald, is again not straightforward for the general reader, and the details can be obtained from his article (Easterlin, 2005). Easterlin essentially shows that there is a 'disjuncture' between evidence obtained from analysis of cross-sectional data and that obtained from analysis of time-series data. More specifically, 'as income increases within the range covered in the cross sectional analysis, happiness fails to reproduce over time its point-of-time relationship to income. Instead of diminishing marginal utility of income, there is zero marginal utility'.

So the claim that the results of happiness research support the postulate of diminishing marginal utility in economic theory has to be treated with very considerable caution. There certainly *are* findings from the happiness literature which do, however, have important implications for economic theory.

Economic theory is in essence a theory about individual

behaviour. It is a theory of how individuals gather information, and the rules they use in processing this information in order to make decisions about allocating scarce resources. In the standard model, people are assumed to obtain all relevant information about a given problem, and then to choose what is for them the best possible decision, the optimal choice. Decision-makers are, in the jargon of economics, 'fully rational'.

If in general this were a true description of behaviour, then the value of much happiness research would be lost. Actual decisions would reliably reveal individuals' preferences. People appear to act as if they want more money, as if they want to consume more goods and services and so on. We would infer from this that having more money made them happier, regardless of the lack of correlation between income and spending and happiness levels measured by the responses of individuals in surveys. True preferences would be revealed by people's actions. By their deeds shall ye know them!

Unfortunately, much of the empirical work in experimental economics over the past couple of decades suggests that we cannot always rely on the assumption that actual decisions and choices accurately reveal preferences. For example, preferences of individuals appear quite frequently to be intransitive. If I prefer product A to B and B to C, then transitive preferences imply that I will prefer A to C. But this is not always the case in practice.[1]

This does not mean that the revealed preferences of consumers have no value. Rather, we must be cautious in how much weight we place on them. This said, preferences revealed by actual choices made by individuals are more likely to be an indicator

---

1   An early article on this is Loomes et al. (1991).

of 'true' preferences than those which are merely stated. So, for example, the revealed preference of millions of people is to shop at Tesco and Sainsbury's, even though their stated preference when interviewed by pollsters is that supermarkets are destroying the small shopkeeper. In politics, in Britain in the 1980s opinion polls showed a strong majority stated a preference for public spending rather than tax cuts. Yet in their actual revealed preferences the electorate chose consistently a political party dedicated to the latter. Furthermore, *either* measure of preference – revealed or stated – has advantages over *ex post* analysis of whether reported happiness seems to correlate with variances in particular goods – an approach currently being proposed for appraisal of environmental policy – as it allows for a more specific, 'higher resolution' understanding of what contributes to and detracts from individuals' welfare. This is examined further in Chapter 6.

More generally, the large literature from behavioural economics and psychology, in which Nobel laureates Daniel Kahneman and Vernon Smith are prominent (see Kahneman, 2002; Smith, 2002), finds consistent problems with the standard economic model of individual behaviour. In general, individuals do not act as if they were maximising utility with fixed preferences and full information.

A key theme in modern economics is that of bounded rationality, introduced by Akerlof and Stiglitz around 1970 (the seminal reference is Akerlof, 1970). People still make what for them is the best possible choice, but they may not have complete information. Furthermore, the information available may vary across decision-makers. But whether the decision-makers are fully or only boundedly rational, they are assumed to operate with fixed tastes and preferences. Each individual takes the decision that is the best for him or her, subject to both the amount of information available and his or her preferences.

Happiness research suggests very strongly that individual preferences are *not* fixed. Instead, they vary over time. The variations may be due to the specific context in which the decision is taken, they may be due to random fluctuations in mood,[2] or they may be due to the longer-term process of adapting to different economic circumstances. Whatever the reason, the key point is that they vary.

And once preferences are allowed to vary over time, the postulate that individuals take the best possible decision given their preferences loses much of its meaning. Is an individual taking a decision now meant to be making the best one given current preferences, or preferences that may or may not come into being at some point in the future?

This certainly does not mean that individuals are not influenced by the set of incentives, both positive and negative, that they face at any point in time. They may still very well act in a self-interested way. What needs to be relaxed is the assumption that they are maximisers, that they always take the best possible decision for them.

In this very particular context, happiness research is a useful part of the modern research programme in economics. Its findings fit in with the wide range of evidence in the more general field of experimental and behavioural economics. In general, economics needs different postulates on individual behaviour from the conventional one of utility maximisation.

---

2   Kahneman and Krueger (2006) cite work that shows, for example, that reported life satisfaction is influenced by the current weather (higher on nice days). Another of their examples is that the answers to a questionnaire on life satisfaction were affected strongly by whether or not a dime was placed at random by the researchers for the subjects to find before they filled it in.

3 HAPPINESS, INCOME AND POLICY

The seminal article in happiness research was published by Richard Easterlin as long ago as 1974 (Easterlin, 1974). He claimed to show that average happiness in the USA had remained at the same level over the period 1946–70, despite the fact that income per head had doubled. These claims are now being advanced more generally for Western economies, for example by Richard Layard of the London School of Economics, a prominent advocate of happiness research (Layard, 2005).

Happiness and national income

The large empirical literature[1] that now exists on happiness has established several propositions. We have already noted these at different points above but, for the sake of clarity, it is useful to list them all together. Their precise quantification varies from study to study, but qualitatively they seem to have very sound support:

1   Happiness is positively correlated with individual income within a given country in any given year; the rich generally report greater happiness than the poor at any given point in time.

---

1   For a register of happiness surveys across 112 countries, for example, see the World Happiness Database (www1.eur.nl/fsw/happiness).

2 But the increase in happiness associated with income within the same country at a point in time appears to get smaller and smaller as income increases.

3 Within an individual country over a number of years, increases in GNP per head over time are associated at best with small increases in happiness, and the majority of studies find no increase at all as GNP increases.

It is important, at the risk of repetition, to clarify the distinction between points (1) and (2) and point (3).

The first two points relate to evidence obtained within a country at a given time. Happiness researchers usually make use of self-reported survey evidence on life satisfaction or wellbeing. The questions can be very simple. For example, the US General Social Survey asks: 'taken all together, how would you say things are these days – would you say that your are: (3) very happy, (2) pretty happy or (1) not too happy'. Di Tella and MacCulloch (2006) plot 1994 mean happiness in the USA against household income per head. Measured on a scale from 1 to 3, the typical increase in happiness from the $10,000–20,000 per head level is 0.09 points, but from the $20,000–30,000 per head level it is 0.05 points. Happiness rises with income, but at a diminishing rate.

The same authors also plot mean happiness and real GDP per head in the USA for each year from 1975 to 1997. Although real GDP per head rises from some $17,000 to around $25,000 over this period, average happiness across the population as a whole is virtually identical in both 1975 and 1997. This illustrates the evidence summarised in point (3) above: happiness appears not to increase over time with GNP.

Some studies do find an increase in happiness over time, but

Figure 1   **UK life satisfaction and GDP, 1973–2002**
            1973 = 100

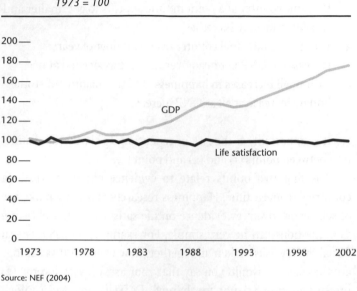

Source: NEF (2004)

this is small. The lack of any marked increase in average happiness is not confined to the high-income countries of the West. Remarkably, a sample of 15,000 individuals interviewed by Gallup in China shows no increase in reported life satisfaction between 1994 and 2005,[2] despite an increase in real income per head of some 150 per cent.

Figure 1 above plots the evidence for the UK, showing 'life satisfaction' (another term for happiness) and real GDP over the period 1973–2002. The chart is taken from a publication by the New Economics Foundation (NEF, 2004).

2   Quoted in Kahneman and Krueger (2006).

In many ways, this is the key evidence on which happiness enthusiasts rely. So we will discuss it at length.

Happiness and life expectancy

Before discussing the happiness data specifically, it is worth noting the work of scholars such as Professor Nick Crafts of the University of Warwick on economic growth and life expectancy (Crafts, 2002). Economic growth promotes life expectancy. More affluent societies do not suffer from malnourishment, people are better clothed and housed, basic provisions such as water and sewage disposal are supplied with much less risk, improved healthcare is affordable, and so on. So, as a result of growth extending life, the lifetime *total* of happiness of an individual will be far greater, even if at any given moment of time he or she may not be happier in a richer society. Since modern life expectancies are almost twice those of Victorian England, this is a quantitatively significant point.

The problems with the happiness data

Moving now to the happiness data, one of the problems in interpreting and drawing conclusions from such data over time is a methodological one. Happiness is often measured in surveys using a three-point scale, where (3) equates to 'very happy'. Higher levels cannot be given as an answer. Given that the average score in such surveys tends to be around 2.2, many respondents must be answering '3'. So even if they were actually reaching higher happiness levels, the survey could not track this.[3]

---

3   The same point applies equally to somewhat more sophisticated surveys which ask people to rate their happiness on a scale from 1 to 10.

With respect to timeline data, the bounded and discrete nature of self-reported happiness also has important implications. First of all, we can usefully ask what a given change in the value of the overall Happiness Index means for individuals. Measuring happiness on the standard three-point scale, the average value in most Western countries is around 2.2. What would actually have to happen to get a 10 per cent increase in happiness, assuming a base happiness of 2.2? We set out the mathematical formula required for this in Appendix 1.

The answer is that there would either have to be 22 per cent (net) of people moving up one category, or 11 per cent of people (net) moving up two categories (or some intermediate mixture of the two). This is quite a large proportion of the population who have to get seriously happy. The long-run average rate of growth in real GDP is in fact around 2.5 per cent, so a 10 per cent increase in this variable usually takes place over a short timescale, on average just four years. It is hardly likely that 22 per cent of the population would achieve a quantum leap in their happiness over a period of only four years.

Trying to base policy on this measure would be like the Monetary Policy Committee of the Bank of England, rather than using GDP as an indicator of the state of the economy, relying instead on a measure that classified people on whether they felt rich, moderately rich or poor. Such an indicator would also no doubt not increase anything like as fast as GDP.

The bounded nature of the happiness data gives rise to further problems when trying to relate it to a variable such as real GDP, which, certainly based on the evidence of the past 200 years, appears able to rise without limit. Over the past twenty years or so there have been major developments in the understanding of correlation and causal links between economic variables over time.[4] A measure of its impact is that two of the principal researchers in this area, Clive Granger and Robert Engel, received the Nobel Prize in 2003.

This literature is large and highly technical. But the relevant point here is that there are potentially very serious problems associated with attempting to deduce correlation and/or causation between a variable such as happiness, which can take values only within strictly defined bounds, and a variable such as real GDP, which can rise without limit. Very little of the happiness literature appears to recognise these problems (a notable exception is the work of Andrew Oswald). A way of trying to illustrate the difficulties, albeit imperfect given the densely mathematical nature of the subject, is as follows. From the average happiness level of around 2.2, the biggest possible increase in the index is some 35 per cent, when literally everyone answers 'very happy' in the happiness survey. If this level were to be reached, even approximately, even if there really were a genuine causal link between real GDP and happiness which operated beyond this point, it could never be identified from the aggregate data. By definition, measured happiness could show no further increase.

There are further fundamental doubts about what timeline happiness data means. In the timeline data, there certainly appears to be no correlation with income per head. But, equally, using the same approach, there is *no* temporal correlation between overall happiness and:

---

4   The seminal article is Engle and Granger (1987).

- increased leisure time;
- crime;
- declining infant mortality;
- increased longevity;
- unemployment;
- declining inequalities between the sexes;
- public spending.

All these things would be expected by any reasonable person to affect happiness. Yet the happiness data over time is to all intents and purposes constant, despite enormous changes in each of the above set of variables. More detailed evidence is provided in Appendix 2, and below we simply mention the evidence. We also note, for completeness, that the use of multiple regression analysis instead of simple two-variable correlations does not alter the conclusion.

Happiness and public expenditure

Public expenditure, whether represented by absolute levels or growth rates, is not correlated over time with happiness. After allowing for inflation, between 1973 and 2004 public spending in the USA almost doubled. In Britain, it rose by 60 per cent. Yet in both countries recorded happiness was a mere 2 per cent higher.

To illustrate the point even more clearly, Figure 2 plots the happiness data from 1973–2002 in the way in which it is used in Figure 1. If we were to rely on happiness data as a basis for policy, what would be the point, one might reasonably ask, of all those schools and hospitals? What would be the point of all those

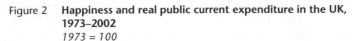

Figure 2   **Happiness and real public current expenditure in the UK,
1973–2002**
1973 = 100

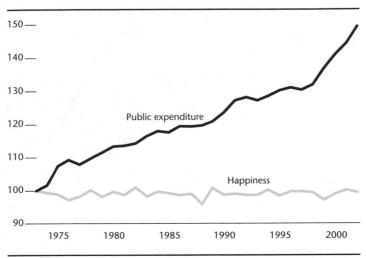

dedicated public servants? More public spending has not led to increases in happiness.[5]

Happiness and social conditions

Moving on to the other variables that one might plausibly believe affect human happiness, leisure time, certainly in Europe, has increased. Between 1979 and 2002, OECD figures (OECD, 2006) show that average annual hours worked in the UK fell by 6 per

---

5   Of course, with regard to public sector, as opposed to private sector, spending, it is possible that the extra spending has not led to much improvement in the quality of the service delivered. This is a separate point but also has uncomfortable implications for those who are the biggest proponents of the happiness research.

Figure 3   **Happiness and the violent crime rate in the USA, 1971–2004**
1971 = 100

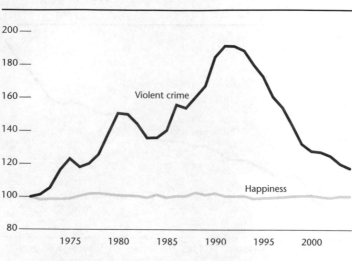

cent. In West Germany the fall was even more marked, by 16 per cent; yet happiness *fell* by 5 per cent over this period.

Crime in European countries is very considerably higher than it was 30 or 40 years ago. Yet this does not seem to have had any discernible negative effect on happiness. Since the early 1990s, crime has fallen noticeably in both the USA and the UK, after very sharp rises over the previous two or three decades. Yet these swings do not register in the happiness data. Figure 3 illustrates this with US data on violent crime and happiness over the period 1971–2004.

So we see that the number of violent crimes per capita almost doubled from 1971 to the early 1990s and has since fallen to a level only 20 per cent higher than in 1971. But these dramatic move-

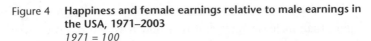

Figure 4   Happiness and female earnings relative to male earnings in
            the USA, 1971–2003
            1971 = 100

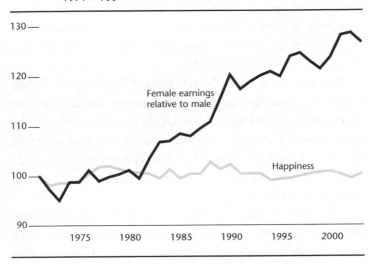

ments are not reflected in any way in the happiness data.

In the USA, life expectancy for whites rose from 72.0 years in 1972 to 78.0 years in 2003. For blacks, the increase was even higher, from 64.6 years to 72.7 years, representing not merely an absolute rise, but a narrowing of the gap with whites. Sex inequality, as measured by the median earnings of women compared with men, has fallen sharply. In 1972, women earned 58 per cent of men's average earnings and this rose to 75 per cent in 2003. But our old friend the happiness time-series pays no attention to these dramatic and desirable social changes. Again for illustration, Figure 4 plots happiness and female earnings relative to male earnings over the period 1971–2003, the latter being the latest year for which reliable estimates are available at the time of writing.

The chart does not mean that female earnings are on average higher than male earnings, but that they have grown faster over the 1971–2003 period, and the differential between the sexes has narrowed. As the chart shows, on average female earnings grew by 30 per cent relative to average male earnings. But, again, this is not reflected in the happiness data.

Of course, this could be rationalised by saying that while women in general had their happiness increased by this, men on average became less happy as a result of the reduction in differentials. But such a rationalisation would merely reveal the subjective nature of happiness. A moral code that suggested that social welfare is higher if women are paid substantially less than men would be barbaric.

The happiness literature does not draw attention to this lack of correlation with a whole range of other variables. Instead, the focus is simply upon the lack of correlation of happiness with income.

Happiness and the distribution of income

The main rationalisation in the happiness literature for the lack of correlation between real GDP and happiness is that it is relative rather than absolute income which is the more important determinant of happiness.

The idea that relative income is important to individuals has been known in economics since the late 1940s, when Duesenberry formulated his relative income hypothesis to explain patterns of income and savings.[6] He observed, for example, that the rich save

---

6   Duesenberry (1948). Duesenberry's brilliant theory accounts much more success-fully for post-war savings patterns than the more orthodox theories of consump-

a bigger proportion of their income than the poor, but national savings do not tend to rise over time despite increases in overall income. He argued that the poor save at lower rates, because the higher spending of others kindles aspirations they find difficult to meet. This difficulty persists no matter how much national income grows, and hence the failure of national savings rates to rise over time. It is immediately apparent that a similar argument could be applied to data on happiness. More generally, the phenomenon of 'keeping up with the Joneses' is very widely attested.

There is, however, no temporal correlation of mean happiness with income inequality. A particular argument made in this context is that taxation should be increased to bring about a more egalitarian society, in which incomes would not be so widely dispersed (Layard, 2005). Yet the happiness data itself does not appear to be related to movements in income inequality. Figure 5 below plots US data for happiness and the Gini coefficient[7] for income inequality. It shows that happiness has both risen and fallen while inequality has increased steadily throughout the period.

If relative income is such a strong determinant of happiness, we would expect to see time-series of reported happiness change clearly with income inequality over time. There is in fact a slight positive correlation between the two, so that the higher levels of inequality over the past 30 years or so tend to be associated with slightly higher levels of happiness. But the correlation is not significant. In the UK also, income inequality has shown some variation over recent decades: for example, it showed a dramatic increase between the early and late 1980s. It is illogical to simultaneously

---

tion in economics, such as the permanent income hypothesis.

7   The Gini coefficient is a standard measure of income inequality. The closer it is to 100, the more unequal is the distribution of income.

Figure 5   **Mean happiness and income inequality (as measured by the Gini coefficient) in the USA, 1971–2004**

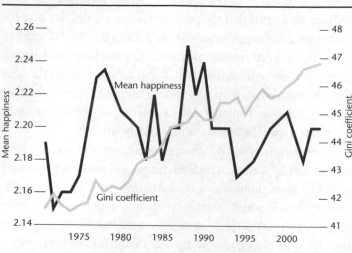

claim that per capita GDP does not affect happiness and use as the explanation for this the fact that it is income inequality which is the important determinant of happiness, when time-series data shows no clear temporal movement in happiness with either of these two variables.

Individuals adapt to expectations and realisable aspirations

Apart from the insensitivity of measures of happiness described above, a convincing explanation for the lack of correlation between happiness and income per head over time is that individuals adapt to changed circumstances.

Stepping aside from economics for a moment, consider the closing scene of George Orwell's great novel *Nineteen Eighty-Four*. Winston Smith, the central character, finally becomes happy. He loves Big Brother. The years of attention devoted to his mental health by the Inner Party member Comrade O'Brien have paid off. A typical *Guardian* reader, forever finding some social problem that renders him outraged, Smith is now content and reconciled with the society in which he lives. And all thanks to the Party and its insight into what constitutes happiness!

Of course, this is fiction, but things just as strange have actually happened. The death of Stalin in 1953 created mass grief throughout the Soviet Union. Contemporary accounts make it clear that this was a genuinely spontaneous outpouring of emotion. And this was for a leader who had created a society based on fear and deceit, in which the living standard of the average citizen was scarcely better than that on offer in the labour camps.

The fictional happiness of Winston Smith and the apparently genuine happiness of many of the citizens of the Soviet Union under Stalin suggest that happiness cannot be separated from its social context. People adapt to their circumstances, and it is possible to be happy in dramatically different contexts. That does not, however, mean that these contexts are equally valid or desirable.

The happiness research we have in the academic literature is largely confined to the experiences of individuals within the Western liberal democracies. But the tendency of individuals to adapt to changes in their circumstances is supported by some of the more serious research within happiness economics itself. Nobel Prize winner Gary Becker, along with Luis Rayo, has recently proposed a 'mean-reverting happiness function that is based on a context-dependent reference point' (Becker and Rayo, 2006). One way of translating this is as follows: happiness depends upon the context in which individuals find themselves, and measured happiness will have a tendency to move back towards its long-run average.

Becker's model is purely theoretical, but a lot of empirical evidence exists for the propositions that happiness depends upon context, and that people adapt to changed circumstances quickly. For example, in psychology Brickman et al. (1978) showed almost thirty years ago that large lottery winners reported comparable life satisfaction levels to non-winners. In terms of adaptation to non-pecuniary changes in life circumstances, such as a deterioration in health, a much more recent study (Oswald and Powdthavee, 2006) found that although the average life satisfaction of people who sustain a moderate disability initially falls, within two years it has recovered completely.

Important contributions from psychology

There is by now a considerable literature on the extent to which the happiness of individuals adapts to changed circumstances over time. Indeed, there is an entire theory in psychology known as 'set point' theory, which maintains that each individual is thought to have a 'set point' of happiness determined by genetics and person-ality. Life events such as marriage, loss of a job and serious injury or disease may deflect a person above or below this set point, but in time adaptation will return an individual to his or her initial level.

As so often with empirical research in the social sciences, not every single result points in the same direction. Easterlin (2003), however, considers a wide range of the literature in a 2003 article in the prestigious American journal *Proceedings of the National Academy of Sciences*. He feels able to draw two conclusions. First, as far as important non-pecuniary changes in individual circumstances are concerned, such as marriage or serious deterioration in health, the set point theory of psychology appears to be refuted rather decisively. Marriage and divorce have a lasting effect on individual happiness, and we return to this important point below.

The second conclusion which Easterlin draws from the literature is, quite simply, that individuals in general *do* adapt to changes in their monetary circumstances. Interesting evidence which he cites includes two of his own papers. These show that when asked how happy they were five years ago, people on average systematically understate their wellbeing at that time. In other words, the happiness levels of individuals are tracked over time, and although on average there is no upward trend despite increases in real incomes, at any point in time individuals contradict their own previous statements and consider that they were less happy five years ago than they are today.

A possible, and entirely sensible, response to this conclusion is that happiness data over time tells us little, if anything, of any practical use in terms of economic policy. In particular, people would adapt to small undramatic improvements in their welfare before those improvements would have an impact on an insensitive aggregate happiness measure. Evidence on adaptation to material circumstances is, however, developed by happiness policy advocates into the so-called 'hedonic treadmill' argument. According to this, the fact that happiness does not increase with economic growth is because people quickly get used to the higher living standards that economic growth brings, to the extent that they are constantly in need of another 'fix' to maintain happiness levels: a phenomenon referred to as the 'hedonic treadmill'.

For example, the Sustainable Development Research Network mentions that: 'as the wealth of individuals and societies increases, they adapt to new, higher living standards and adjust expectations upwards. This "hedonic adaptation" means that aspirations are never satisfied, and that "increasing pleasure is needed to maintain a steady state of wellbeing"' (SDRN, 2006). Layard (2005) posits that 'the secret of happiness is to seek out those good things that you can never fully adapt to', and suggests that the phenomenon is analogous to nicotine and alcohol addiction, thereby requiring higher taxes on income for our own good – just as politicians try to tax us to reduce the incentive to become addicted to nicotine and alcohol.

While it is reasonable to suggest that the relentless pursuit of material possessions might not be the route to happiness, there are two key criticisms of the 'hedonic adaptation' argument. The first relates to its underlying assumption that something is not worth doing if the pleasure or interest that it initially stimulates cannot be sustained. But this is the norm, not the exception, in a vast array of human experiences. The fulfilment of many aspirations and ambitions at some point no longer engenders the same excitement that was once expected by the person wishing for them. The intense passion of falling in love is not (always) sustained through 60 years of marriage; the excitement of being offered a longed-for job wears off with the daily routine of hard work, stress and commuting; representing your county athletics club in competition is no longer an honour once one has one's heart set on an Olympic medal.

The fact that the emotions that spur people to achieve these aspirations may eventually wear off or be superseded by higher ambition is not an argument for not seeking to fulfil them: they are stages leading on to better things, and they have impacts on other people – in other words, they have a value beyond the transitory emotional state of the protagonist. Indeed, some deep-seated satisfaction may well come out of striving for the next goal – even if people do not regard that satisfaction as the same emotion as happiness.

Second, it is not explicitly clear what the 'hedonic adaptation' observations suggest for public policy. It seems to be implicit in the argument that a steady-state economy, or at least one with low growth, would be better than a quickly growing economy, because people would have less to habituate to and would suffer less disappointment. But if it is axiomatic that whatever makes people happy is the ultimate moral end, and a process is observed to make people happier for a while, then surely it would be more valid to argue that the process should be continued at a level at which the 'wearing-off' periods are minimised than to argue that the process should not happen at all?

The hedonic adaptation argument is effectively saying that happiness is a function of the rate of economic growth; if this rate is below a certain critical level, then increases in happiness will not occur continuously over time, but will occur only in fits and starts and will be prone to reversal. Assuming for one moment that it were possible to fine-tune the rate of economic growth, if one accepts that happiness is the goal of economic policy, it would make more sense to argue that economic growth should be at or above this critical level rather than zero.

So the implied 'low economic growth' policy argument based

on the concept of hedonic adaptation is logically inconsistent. This is because it is based on an insistence that people should experience only 'the right type' of happiness, rather than an acceptance that if happiness is the overall objective of policy, it is not the policymaker's place to pick and choose which emotional states most resemble a correct definition.

In summary, the time-series data on happiness seems to contain very little genuine information. Individuals adjust rapidly to changed circumstances, so there is not an absolute standard of happiness. And the data appears to be uncorrelated with a wide range of both 'goods' and 'bads', such as income inequality, leisure and mortality. There are therefore very serious doubts over the robustness of time-series data, about the inferences made from it and their use as a basis for policy, as well as grave doubts about the potential for an official 'Happiness Index' or measure of 'gross national happiness', which is further discussed in Chapter 5. Despite these shaky foundations, the relative income happiness hypothesis, as we might call it, has nevertheless been seized upon for policy recommendations.[8]

What does affect happiness?

In contrast to the above, the happiness literature provides evidence on various factors that *do* seem to contribute to or detract from the happiness of individuals. Non-timeline data shows that, generally, stable family life, being married, financial security, health, having religious faith, feelings of living in a cohesive community where people can be trusted, and good governance contribute to happi-

---

8   An interesting critique of the conventional recommendations of happiness research can be found in Wilkinson (2007).

HAPPINESS, INCOME AND POLICY

ness. Chronic pain, divorce, unemployment and bereavement detract from happiness.[9]

The evidence on marriage is especially impressive, as is noted above. The purely economic benefits of marriage have been established for some considerable time. For example, 25 years ago Gary Becker argued that, at its most basic, there are economies of scale within a household (Becker, 1981). More recently, a number of empirical studies have shown that, even after taking into account other relevant factors, on average married individuals earn more than single people (for example, Loh, 1996). There is now a large literature on the physiological and psychological benefits of marriage. Married people show better physical health, longevity, psychological health and reported happiness. A valuable survey of these findings is contained in Wilson and Oswald (2005).

This survey is particularly useful because it focuses on the studies from which the most reliable inferences can be drawn. A difficult problem, which is general to many empirical issues in economics, lies in disentangling the causality between two factors, in this context marriage and wellbeing. Marriage may promote wellbeing but, equally, individuals who are prone for whatever reason to exhibit high levels of wellbeing may be more likely to become married (for example, they presumably make more attractive potential mates).

The use of what is known as panel, or longitudinal, data is recognised in statistics and econometrics as offering methodologically the best way of dealing with this issue. Panel data combines both cross-sectional data and time-series data. So such a data set will have information about individuals at a point in time, and it

---

9   For example, Diener and Suh (1999); Frey and Stutzer (2002b).

will also follow such individuals through time. It is not a panacea, but is thought to be the best way of approaching the inherently challenging problems of causality.

The Wilson and Oswald survey considers only results that are obtained from the analysis of panel data. They reference no fewer than 95 papers drawn from a variety of disciplines. The results are striking:

- Marriage makes people far less likely to suffer psychological illness.
- Marriage makes people live much longer.
- Marriage makes people healthier and happier.
- Both men and women benefit, though some investigators have found that men gain more.
- These gains are not merely because married people engage in less risky activities.
- Marriage quality and prior beliefs can influence the size of the gains.

Moreover, not only are the benefits confined to those who are married rather than cohabiting, but they are large. In terms of health, for example, the longevity effect of marriage may even offset the consequences of smoking.

So, insofar as policy conclusions can be drawn at this stage of happiness research, they imply increased support for marriage, reductions in incentives to single parents, and the promotion of religious faith in various ways. This is not a set of policy conclusions that most proponents of the happiness research tend to emphasise.

4 HAPPINESS AND MACROECONOMICS

A distinct strand in happiness research claims that macro-economic policy has a strong effect on the happiness of nations.[1] For example, several studies examine how much happiness is reduced by increases in both inflation and unemployment, and use the results to suggest better policies. Increases in both these variables allegedly reduce happiness. It is argued that by quantifying these reductions, governments can be better informed about the consequences of the trade-off they can make between inflation and unemployment – the so-called Phillips curve. *If* governments both understand the quantitative trade-off between inflation and unemployment and are able to control both these variables, then a mix could be chosen which leads to the least unhappiness.

We have to say that such arguments have a quaintly old-fashioned air about them, harking back to the days before Milton Friedman's devastating attack as long ago as 1968 on the existence and stability of the Phillips curve trade-off. The idea that there is a trade-off between inflation and unemployment which governments understand is one that has been discredited in serious macroeconomics for almost forty years.

But the problems with the happiness policy argument in this context go farther. For example, even within happiness research

---

1   For example, Di Tella et al. (2003), Di Tella and MacCulloch (2006) and the articles cited in these papers.

itself, the trade-off between inflation and unemployment 'varies between different studies' (Di Tella and MacCulloch, 2006). So governments looking to use any such finding would first of all have to decide which estimated trade-off to use.

This lack of consensus is entirely typical of results in applied macroeconomics. For example, there has been a programme of research into macroeconomic modelling for over thirty years, yet the policy properties of the models are if anything even more different from each other today than they were 30 years ago.[2]

Moreover, as any economic forecaster knows, macroeconomic relationships break down much more frequently and more spectacularly than statistical, econometric theory suggests. Unlike academics who publish an article on, say, the consumption function, and then go on to something else, forecasters are obliged to confront their equations on a regular basis with genuine out-of-sample data.

In addition, the track record of macroeconomic forecasting is poor by scientific standards, and shows no sign of improving over time. In order to make policy changes now which will improve the outturn of the economy, say, one year ahead, governments need to have predictions that are reasonably accurate over time. Without an accurate assessment of where the economy is likely to be in the immediate future, it is not possible to decide in any meaningful way on how policy should be altered at any given time. The forecasts, it should be said, are especially unreliable at anticipating recessions, and it is precisely during a recession that unemployment is likely to rise sharply.

The breakdown of macroeconomic relationships is not due

---

2   Perhaps the first systematic comparison of UK macro-model properties is Laury et al. (1978).

to faulty econometrics, but due to inherent features of the data. Macroeconomic data in general contains very little genuine information and is more akin to series that are random than to series that have any systematic structure. Modern signal processing techniques demonstrate this very clearly. An explanation of this in everyday English would require several pages and take us far beyond the main purpose of this monograph. Interested readers are referred to Ormerod and Mounfield (2000).

In short, the view that governments can both predict and control short-term movements in the economy has proved to be an illusion rather than reality. In particular, the idea that a deterioration in one variable can be systematically traded against an improvement in another is simply not credible. Controlling happiness by controlling macroeconomic policy is impossible.

5 'GROSS NOTIONAL HAPPINESS': MEASUREMENT AND DECISION-MAKING

One of the policy recommendations given by Richard Layard in his influential book *Happiness: Lessons from a New Science* (Layard, 2005) is that 'we should monitor the development of happiness as closely as we monitor the development of income'. Indeed, in the UK there are currently moves to create a detailed set of national 'wellbeing accounts', which, it is argued, will help government better understand how wellbeing changes over time. Furthermore, the academic advisers to the Whitehall Wellbeing Working Group argue for 'clear wellbeing targets with appropriate incentives designed to meet those targets' to enhance policy success (Dolan et al., 2006).

In policymaking circles and political debate, however, numbers and statistics can take on lives of their own, so it is vital that they contain real information that is easy to interpret correctly. In Chapter 3 we examined how, despite the fact that measured happiness seems to show that 60 years of economic and political labours of all descriptions have made no difference to the welfare of the citizens of the Western world, bold policy recommendations have already been based on a selective interpretation of the data. The concern is then that happiness data might be used without sufficient caveats and awareness of any inherent limitations, and that this would detract from, rather than aid, policymaking. In this chapter, we discuss this possibility in comparison with GNP and some of its variants.

There have been many criticisms of GNP, prominent among which is the fact that it does not account for factors that detract from people's welfare but which may be stimulated by economic growth, such as pollution or commuting. Indeed, sometimes GNP will increase because of activities that *reduce* welfare. Happiness research is merely the latest in the long line of criticisms of the concept of GNP.

The concept of gross national product[1] did not really take off as a policymaking tool until the 1930s and 1940s. The driving force behind the measurement of the size of the economy was the Harvard economist Simon Kuznets, awarded the Nobel Prize in 1971. Unlike many Nobel laureates, Kuznets believed very firmly that economics had to be an empirical science.

In part, the inspiration for measuring GNP was Keynesian economics. If, as Keynes believed, the government can influence and partly control short-term fluctuations in the economy, then it is sensible to construct a systematic way of measuring the size of the economy. In this way, we can formalise what is happening, whether the economy is growing or contracting.

In any event, *the* principal economic concern of the 1930s was the stupendous collapse in output that had taken place in the early years of the decade. Unsurprisingly, the first systematic attempts to measure the economy were concerned with what was being spent and produced – in short, with GNP.

But the originators of GNP never insisted that this was the *only* way of measuring an economy. In his Nobel lecture, for

---

1   In the UK, gross domestic product (GDP) is the more widely used concept. The differences between GDP and GNP are usually very small, GNP being the somewhat more general of the two concepts.

example, Kuznets specifically discussed the social implications of growth and argued that: 'Many of these are of particular interest, because they are not reflected in the current measures of economic growth; and the increasing realization of this short-coming of the measures has stimulated lively discussion of the limits and limitations of economic measurement of economic growth' (Kuznets, 1971).

Indeed, a great deal of the work to extend the concept of GNP over the past 30 years or so has been carried out by economists. A seminal paper in 1972 by Bill Nordhaus and James Tobin introduced the concept of the 'Measure of Economic Welfare' (Nordhaus and Tobin, 1972). They extended the definition of GNP by adding estimates for the value of leisure time and some non-market production, and by deducting some of the costs associated with urbanisation, such as commuting. They also excluded from GNP any spending on the police and defence, which they argued did not contribute to economic welfare.

This latter point highlights the inescapable arbitrariness of measuring the economy, whether in terms of output or wellbeing. Many people might choose to include at least part of defence and police spending, for example, on the grounds that state-enforced security of citizens does contribute to their welfare.

Much more substantial adjustments are made to GNP in the Index of Sustainable Economic Welfare (ISEW) (Daly and Cobb, 1989). The index attempts to incorporate both environmental effects and changes in the distribution of income. For example, an identical increase in GNP measured in the conventional sense is regarded as leading to a smaller increase in ISEW if it is associated with a widening of the income distribution, or with greater environmental pollution, than if it is not.

The ISEW has been particularly influential, since it first created a concern that increasing GNP might not be the principal aim of economic policy. For example, between 1950 and 1990 real GNP per capita in the USA rose by just over 100 per cent, but initial estimates of ISEW showed an increase of only 16 per cent. The ISEW appeared to have fallen during the 1980s.

Because of the sheer number of components added and subtracted from the ISEW (and the fact that many of the assumptions used to calculate it are without empirical foundation), however, it is almost tailor made for prejudiced interpretation. For example, the fact that it rises to a peak and then declines has been automatically interpreted by certain NGOs as showing that any recent gains in material welfare have been offset by increased income inequality and environmental deterioration. In fact, the decline is almost entirely attributable to decreases in unpaid household labour, which the ISEW adds to GDP[2] (another arbitrary decision, as many people probably feel better off doing less housework). But one would have to examine the original data oneself in order to know that. Great familiarity with the index is needed in order to separate out the different strands of information it contains in order to interpret it. In other words, it confuses rather than effectively summarises disparate information.

This discussion is relevant because it illustrates how easy it is for measures and indicators that have acquired an air of rigour and objectivity to be unquestioningly given a biased interpretation.

More generally, measures should not be separated from the decisions they are used to inform; the use of a measure depends

2   See the discussion in Chapter 17 of Perman et al. (1999).

on its ability to guide decision-making. In other words, with every proposed indicator, it is useful to consider in advance what political action changes in the indicator might stimulate, and vice versa. If use of GNP is leading to sub-optimal decisions, greater specificity over where and how would be useful in clarifying how this could be rectified.

Increasing a measure is naturally not the same, however, as increasing whatever it is supposed to be measuring, as the literally incredible recent increases in GCSE and A-level passes and grades illustrates. Centralised systems of maximising indicators and setting targets increase the remoteness of those making decisions from those affected by them, reducing feedback, introducing perverse incentives and making decisions more vulnerable to poor-quality information. The more complex and subjective the concept, the truer this is. The suggestion that policies should be designed to meet wellbeing targets therefore raises the prospect of a dysfunctional relationship between policymakers and reality. Given the measurement problems already described, much happiness data is indeed of poor quality with a low information content. Any increase shown by hypothetical official happiness measures would probably be fortuitous for the prevailing administration, rather than the result of policy, while any decrease could well generate media pressure for unjustified new initiatives. This new vehicle for crediting or blaming government for things it has done or not done would erode the process of assessing policies based on a rational and empirical establishment of relationships between cause and effect – and is unlikely to encourage better government.

In general, much of the thought surrounding alternative measures of prosperity seems to be based on an implicit assumption that the economy works by measuring things and directing resources accordingly. For example, SDRN (2006) notes that some environmentalists argue for the inclusion of 'the value of domestic labour and caring work' in national accounts as 'only then will we have sustainable community life with high levels of wellbeing'. All we need to do is 'measure what matters' and the correct responses will cascade through successive layers of government unhindered by information problems, administrative glitches, political constraints or competing priorities.

This emphasis on gathering information and modifying or supplementing GNP as a means towards more wellbeing-enhancing policies seems based on an overestimation of the degree of control the government is able to exercise in the economy and society. There is little recognition in such statements that liberal economies do not work by central gathering and processing of information, but by short-cutting the need to collect it altogether, by allowing agents to act in their own economic interest independently of central control.

The economy would not grind to a halt if GNP were not measured at all for a couple of years, as indeed it was not before the 1930s. An illustration of this is Hong Kong, where John Cowperthwaite, a British colonial administrator in the post-war period, not only introduced free market polices but in his years as financial secretary (1961–71) refused to collect economic statistics at all for fear that this would only give government officials an excuse for more meddling. And while at the end of World War II Hong Kong was a very poor island with a per capita income about one quarter that of Britain's, by 1997, when sovereignty was transferred to China, its per capita income was roughly equal to that of the departing colonial power.

There is little discussion in many proposals for modifying GNP, or alternatively measuring wellbeing, of how political decisions would actually be made better as a result of different accounting practices.[3] It is not clear which government decisions or actions would be enhanced, either on a local or a national scale, by including the value of domestic labour in national accounts, for example. Furthermore, there do not appear to date to have been any decisions in UK central government which have been made differently because of information provided by environmental accounts. Arguments for modifying or supplementing government indicators should be firmly rooted in the context of the decisions they will influence, otherwise they risk becoming simulacrums of action, endlessly proposed but to no particular end. Any political decision can be informed by appropriate data (for example, data on income distributions), but we do not need a summary measure that purports to summarise all contributions to welfare in a well-being indicator.

One of the noted names in the happiness literature, Nobel laureate Daniel Kahneman, recently argued (Kahneman, 2006) that national accounts based on self-reported happiness would not be a useful aid to government decision-making, and that any difference policymakers could make on influencing happiness would be 'marginal'. It is sobering to hear someone so closely associated with the research reach such a conclusion, and those who believe that wellbeing accounts are necessary might do well to question why.

---

3   The exception to this is the measure of 'Genuine Savings' used by the World Bank, which adjusts GNP for changes to natural capital stocks. It is more rigorously defined than the ISEW and has been used to advise some developing countries on strategies for natural resource management. See, e.g., Hamilton and Clemens (1999).

For all its faults, at least GNP is well defined, based on something that is already quantified and bears some readily verifiable relationship to reality. Its rough order of magnitude and direction of change can be cross-checked with objective reality – for example, we observe that when GNP decreases, people *do* suffer relative economic hardship, and tax receipts go down. Proposed methods of redress – such as tax cuts or interest rate changes – are transparent and open to empirical appraisal. The indicator has proven and predictable (within reason) causal relationships with respect to both economic and some social trends and policy interventions. It can be accurately updated and consistently compared across time. There is less confusion of disparate information and no adaptation. It is continuous, not discrete, so that small gradual improvements are recorded. Further, increases over time *are* correlated with 'goods' such as reduced infant mortality, increased longevity and reductions in sex inequality.

By contrast, it is difficult to see how a measure of happiness could bear the properties of cross-verifiability and objective interpretation required for policy diagnosis and prescription. These are surely prerequisites for any indicator's ability to add to, rather than obfuscate, effective decision-making at a national level.

Central to this question is clarity over how GNP is currently used in decision-making, how much this affects economic growth, and how much economic growth would happen anyway as the result of undirected efforts. Many of the factors associated with economic growth which are thought to decrease happiness (e.g. commuting) seem to be the unintended by-products of undirected decisions, rather than the foreseen and accepted downsides of carefully formulated plans. The suggestion that they would be remedied by using an alternative measure of prosperity to GNP massively oversimplifies the causation of political decision-making, and glosses over the concerted political programme, no doubt with downsides and unintended consequences of its own, which would be required to keep them in check.

The economy is not an object in the physical sciences which can be put in a pair of scales and weighed. Whatever metric is chosen, definitions of what is and is not excluded have to be made and a whole variety of sources used to make the estimates. This point applies just as much to GNP, as familiarity with how national accounts are constructed in practice makes clear.[4] But a measure that does not act as an uncluttered aid to lucid decision-making is worse than useless; it is a drag on our political system.

---

4   See, for example, Maurice (1968).

6 APPLICATIONS OF HAPPINESS RESEARCH

It is reasonable to argue that preferences revealed in markets are incomplete indicators of welfare (even setting to one side problems associated with, for example, non-transitivity of preferences discussed in Chapter 2 above). First, questions of resource allocation are largely irrelevant to some of the factors that seem to make people happy, such as religious belief. Second, where questions of resource allocation are relevant, goods and services exchanged in markets represent only a subset of those that contribute to people's happiness. Therefore, relying on indicators of preferences revealed in markets as a sole indicator of welfare would be misleading.

Assessment of the value of environmental goods

Environmental goods such as clean air and landscape are a particularly important category of goods that contribute to welfare but which are outside the scope of markets. Given that many such goods can only be publicly provided or protected,[1] and the fact that there is no equivalent of price signalling their value, the anguished question of how to assess the impact on

---

1   That is not to say that ways could not be conceived of having private markets in environmental goods to a greater extent, but that is a debate separate from the point we are making, which is based on the realities of the situation in the UK.

welfare of such goods in government policies is continually pondered.

One might get the impression from some of the wellbeing literature, however, that this is not the case. For example, NEF (2004) writes that: 'By focusing purely on economic indicators, we have missed the negative side effects of economic growth and efficiency. These might include the depletion of environmental resources, the stress from working long hours, and the unravelling of local economies and communities.'

It is highly misleading to imply that, prior to the interest in wellbeing research, the impact of environmental 'goods' and 'bads' on social welfare had been ignored by policymakers. In fact the UK government has been incorporating environmental 'non-market' factors into policy decisions for some years. The official government guidelines on policy appraisal, the Treasury's *Green Book*, clearly state that: 'wider social and environmental costs and benefits for which there is no market price also need to be brought into any [policy] assessment' and that 'the valuation of non-market impacts is a challenging but important element of appraisal, and should be attempted wherever feasible' (HMT, 2003).

Evidence on the value that people place on non-market goods is teased out both by examining their behaviour and by asking them about their preferences. Examining how green space affects house prices is an example of the former (and uses revealed preferences), while the creation of hypothetical markets ('how much *would* you pay to maintain this good?') is an example of the latter (stated preferences).

The metric used to assess and trade off non-market benefits is money. This is not because economists imagine people to be particularly venal or materialistic, but because it is thought that people are well practised in assessing how highly disparate things contribute to their welfare through this means. For example, imagine someone who takes pleasure in the natural beauty of mountains in winter conditions. We might reasonably infer that the time and money he or she spends on accommodation, travel and mountaineering equipment, for example, can be used directly as a component of the measure of the value placed by the individual on this beauty compared with other goods or activities that he or she could spend time and money on.

Further, the use of the money metric introduces a budget constraint and ensures that trade-offs in competing resource uses are incorporated; if people really value something, then they should be prepared to forgo something else in order to obtain it. These methods do have their limitations, however. For example, the use of hypothetical markets is flawed when outcomes of decisions are non-deterministic or subject to highly uncertain human agency.

'New' approaches to the assessment of the value of environmental goods

The use of wellbeing research has been proposed to supplement or replace this approach to appraisal of environmental policies and to inform resource allocation decisions (Dolan and Peasgood, 2006). This would mark a shift away from using people's preferences as an indicator of their welfare, to an *ex post* analysis of what appears to have made them happier. It would involve gathering data on self-reported wellbeing and regressing it against the abundance of environmental goods and other explanatory factors, to derive a relationship between the environmental good in question and wellbeing. The results would then be converted into monetary values by comparison with the statistical effect that income has on self-reported wellbeing. But this approach brings its own problems. By its very nature, it cannot be used to evaluate processes that have not yet happened, or have not been noticed; which affect everyone equally (e.g. carbon dioxide emissions or the extinction of a species); or which cause only momentary blips in mood.

The latter point can be illustrated by the case of nutrient pollution. It is extremely unlikely that a meaningful correlation would be found between reported happiness levels and nutrient pollution, which causes overgrowth of plant life in water bodies, thereby starving the water of oxygen. Yet surely most people walking by a stream would rather see fish, ducklings and dragon-flies than uniform green scum. Asking them whether this is indeed the case – despite there being other private and public spending priorities – would be more likely to provide evidence to make the case for mitigating nutrient pollution than using information from reported happiness studies.

Ex post analysis would be more susceptible to biases due to simultaneity and missing variables in regression analysis. For example, would people be less happy in areas of high air pollution because of the pollution itself, or because of factors such as the ugliness of traffic and industrial infrastructure, which are strongly correlated with high levels of pollution? Furthermore, percep-tions may not be equivalent to reality. A study of noise levels near Schiphol Airport found that reported wellbeing was correlated with *perceived* but not *physically recorded* noise (Van Praag, 2004). Possibly only people who were already stressed or anxious partic-ularly noticed the noise. This does not mean, however, that other people in the area would not like a reduction in noise, or that an intervention to reduce noise would necessarily make the unhappier folk happier.

This seems to suggest that seeking evidence on actual preferences allows a greater specificity in examining what does and does not contribute to individuals' welfare – and a 'higher resolution' of understanding – than an *ex post* analysis of whether they are happier. As explained in Chapter 3, small, gradual improvements in welfare would be likely to have little impact on measured happiness. Many environmental improvements are too small to affect reported happiness levels, but may nevertheless be desirable.

Health and happiness

Further problems can be imagined with respect to assessing health priorities. Happiness policy advocates are particularly keen on spending to try to cure depression and mental illness. For example, the *Depression Report* published by the Centre for Economic Performance at the London School of Economics in June 2006 claims that no fewer than one in six of the adult population of the UK currently suffers from mental illness attributable to depression or 'chronic anxiety disorder'. The signatories call for the training of 10,000 additional therapists, 'according to a 7-year Plan centrally funded and commissioned'. (Gosplan,[2] thou shouldst be living at this hour!)

How might we assess this demand compared with, say, spending an equal amount on the physically disabled or the

---

2   The Central Planning Bureau of the defunct Soviet Union.

sight-impaired? Certainly, the happiness literature suggests that these latter groups should have low priority. In his 2006 *Journal of Economic Perspectives* article cited earlier, economics Nobel Prize winner Daniel Kahneman notes that disability, even of a severe form, does not have a strong long-term effect on reported levels of life satisfaction. Indeed, following the onset of moderate disability, average life satisfaction fully recovers to the pre-disability level within two years.

The idea that preventing disability should receive a lower priority than treating depression might not be one that is acceptable to everyone. Happiness research does not absolve us from the need to make judgements on priorities. Some may very well feel that, for example, while depression can be very debilitating, it is at least reversible and, with a bit of luck, it can be overcome without professional help. It is certainly questionable whether resources for its treatment should be prioritised over preventing irreversible paralysis and blindness.

As it happens, the LSE depression report does not provide evidence that the overall level of recorded happiness is affected by rises in depression. And, indeed, recorded measures of depression have increased markedly in recent years (at least treatment has), while average recorded happiness has not fallen.

Other policy dilemmas

There are two questions routinely faced in policy appraisal which happiness economics is yet to address. The first is the question of the inter-temporal allocation of resources and the timing of the benefits brought about by policies. The second is the question of assessing trade-offs between the outcomes of different policy options.

Policies have different timescales and different start dates. For example, a policymaker may have two alternative policies, one of which will start yielding benefits straight away, the second of which will start yielding higher benefits five years from now.[3] Policy appraisal has to make an explicit choice about which of these is preferable, based on assumptions on whether we prefer to have our benefits up front or delayed: in other words, it has to take inter-temporal preferences into account.

Happiness economics is at too early a stage to have thoroughly developed techniques to deal with inter-temporal choices. As discussed above, there are some clues on inter-temporal preferences in the happiness literature: actions that increase happiness only temporarily are discouraged, as 'overall life satisfaction' is the aim. There is little guidance, however, on how temporary the increase in happiness from a policy would have to be before it would not be worth pursuing: a week, a year, ten years? Formal policy appraisal would need a way of deciding this.

Furthermore, there are no clues as to how the magnitude of an effect is to be traded against its duration. There is no discussion of whether a policy that makes 1 per cent of people happier over ten years is better than one that makes 0.5 per cent of people happier over twenty years. It may seem slightly ridiculous to even discuss figures in this manner, but these are the kinds of decisions that need to be informed by a measure of welfare which should, according to its proponents, be used to make policy decisions.

As with all methods and metrics, use of wellbeing data has the potential to throw up anomalous and questionable results. Some

---

3   Indeed, with regard to policies on pensions and the environment – or even decisions relating to the size of the government budget deficit – the costs and benefits may be separated by a generation or more.

of those who have popularised wellbeing research (e.g. NEF, 2004) continue to give the misleading impression that environmental benefits are not already taken into account in policymaking, thus exaggerating the moral case for the wellbeing agenda. In fact there do not appear to be any publicly available studies that demonstrate that a specific environmental policy decision would have been better made if approaches proposed in the happiness literature had been used instead of current approaches.

Indeed, Dolan et al. (2006) suggest that a priority for researching the link between environmental policy and wellbeing is to ascertain whether infrastructure projects of the type objected to by 'Not In My Backyard' campaigners actually reduce the subjective wellbeing of those who object in the long term. If it were found that people living near infrastructure projects did not have their happiness reduced, it can be imagined that some might take this as justification for dismissing their views more readily. As with the application of much happiness research, this would have interesting implications for the liberal democratic processes that are usually used to settle such matters, as those who purported to centralise the information about other people's happiness could use that information to justify imposing their solution.

In fact, given that government policy appraisal already does include environmental and other non-market benefits, the dichotomy that the use of wellbeing research throws up is not that of a holistic versus a materialistic conception of welfare; rather, it is between accepting individual preferences as a reasonable indicator of welfare and not doing so.

7 FINAL REMARKS AND CONCLUSIONS

Politics sometimes gives rise to concepts that seem so open and uncontroversial that people automatically assume that they encapsulate diverse political aims that they already see as inherently good. For example, Hayek said of the phrase 'the common good' that: 'it does not need much reflection to see that [this term has] no sufficiently definite meaning to determine a particular course of action'. Yet people of all political persuasions automatically use it to justify whatever policies they subjectively believe to be the right ones.

Similarly, many people automatically assume that happiness-based policy would advance causes that they already champion, such as environmental protection or social justice. We saw in the previous chapter, however, that there does not appear to be any evidence that happiness-based environmental policy would offer improvements to current practice.[1] Conversely, there are areas where happiness arguments or evidence might produce or camouflage morally questionable outcomes. This highlights not only that not everything can be reduced to its effects on empirically observed happiness, but that it will always be a political and moral call as to what happiness evidence is acceptable, throwing into doubt its use as an objective measure.

---

1   A recent report to the Whitehall Wellbeing Working Group acknowledges that 'there is very little evidence on the relationship between sustainability and SWB [subjective wellbeing]' (Dolan et al., 2006).

For example, at least one country in the world has decided that cultural homogeneity is a vital part of its citizens' happiness. The Kingdom of Bhutan, for example, is cited approvingly by leading happiness advocates for being the first country in the world to use the concept of gross national happiness as the basis for policy. In this fortunate nation, national dress is compulsory and, until recently, television was banned.

A further way in which the government of Bhutan is promoting happiness is not mentioned in the literature. Bhutan wants to protect and maintain its culture, so the government achieves this by expelling the minority of the population which is ethnically Nepalese. Many Nepalese are confined to camps in the southern part of the country and their children have restricted access to education or are denied it altogether. Any person who is 'un-Bhutanese' can be asked to leave the country, and reports of torture and illegal imprisonment are widespread. In short, in Bhutan 'happiness' is being promoted by ethnic cleansing. Such a policy appears to be very popular, judged by the frequency with which we observe it in world history.

A less dramatic but nevertheless important illustration is provided by some of the studies on happiness and income inequality, which seem to suggest that it is only income within peer groups – among groups of people with whom one compares oneself – which determines happiness, rather than income inequality in society as a whole.[2] One could deduce from this that a society in which social classes are relatively static, where people befriend only those in a similar income bracket, and where nobody tries to improve their status or wealth relative to their peers, might

2   Cited in Kahneman and Krueger (2006).

be less prone to anxiety and discontent than a more socially fluid, meritocratic model.[3] But the moral distaste most people would feel if we were to actively aim for such a society would override any such arguments.

The reason why happiness research has touched a chord is valid. It is entirely reasonable not to want to live in a society totally dominated by commercial or material concerns. It is entirely reasonable to want a feeling of values shared with one's fellow citizens, and to feel that both you and they are not entirely driven by pure self-interest. The interest that happiness research has sparked is a manifestation of these aspirations. Adam Smith noted all these things, but he also sketched out how they could be achieved more effectively in society without using the political apparatus to impose policy but relying on the voluntary cooperation of individuals and communities.

The application of happiness economics to policy would take empiricism in public policymaking to an extreme level. Happiness economics effectively argues that we need only one value in our society – that of maximising *measured* happiness – and that all other values are subordinated to this end. All that we need do is demonstrate the causal link between each action and its effects on happiness to decide whether it is 'good' or 'bad'. In that way, we can remove the need for any other value judgement.

We cannot rely on empirical evidence to prove everything; it is costly to gather and is often – even by trained academics – misinterpreted. Much of the work on happiness and wellbeing in public policy seems to be trying to prove things that we knew all along – that a stable family life and having access to green space

---

3   See, for example, de Botton (2004) for a description of the anxiety and fear of failure that meritocracy creates.

is good for you. The fact that people now feel compelled to make a detailed technocratic supplication to the centre to support even these most basic inclinations is not progress. Rather, if public agencies are busy demonstrating that 'green space has wellbeing benefits' in order to make the case for, say, local playing fields, this indicates a loss of control at a local level over the factors that people judge to affect their happiness.

There are very many things that both happiness research and common sense would expect to have affected (for good or ill) the contentment of citizens in Western societies over the past 60 years. The fact that they appear not to have done so suggests either that even trying to increase the sum total of human happiness is an exercise in monumental futility, or that there are serious problems with measuring happiness.

Certainly, it seems a case of choosing one's evidence to fit one's argument to claim that only *one* particular change – increased material living standards – is the single overwhelming factor primarily responsible for making no difference whatsoever to recorded happiness. We might have expected the huge increase in leisure time in the second half of the twentieth century, say, or the high unemployment of the 1980s, or the rise in government spending on health and education, to have had an impact on happiness time-series. They did not.

The development and use of a happiness indicator for policy purposes is inconceivable until internal consistency within the data has been shown: i.e. that if a particular social or economic variable is believed to affect happiness, and it changes substantially over time, a commensurate effect on time-series data is identified.

If economists do not clearly communicate what economic growth is for, they should not be surprised if people read their position to be one that equates the freedom to consume with happiness, nor that there is distaste for such a world-view, and an appetite for any analysis, no matter how badly thought through, which purports to refute it. The dichotomy presented by many proponents of happiness research, however – that the use of GNP implies a narrow, materialistic and self-centred view of welfare, while use of 'gross national happiness' (or wellbeing) would imply a more holistic or ethical conception – is a false one. GNP clearly does not measure happiness, but its usefulness within the limited scope of economic decision-making is clear.[4]

As Chapter 6 mentions, arguably the real dichotomy is not that of a material versus a holistic conception of welfare; it is between accepting preferences as a useful indicator of welfare, despite the acknowledged flaws of such an approach, and not doing so. In its political form, this boils down to a decision whether to accept that people's own judgement of what is good for them can be trusted. Once people are officially viewed as having little capacity to decide correctly on small matters related to their own welfare, their supposedly weak judgements can be more readily dismissed. The logical conclusion of much happiness research – that individuals' own judgements about what is good for them can be overridden by experts wielding clipboards and regression models – is illiberal, undemocratic and unattractively paternalistic.

The more responsibility government accrues the more of its record it has to defend. The more it has to defend, the more it will be tempted to influence the way this record is presented. Happiness evidence, with its track record of subjective interpretation, its lack of objective verifiability on a macro level and the likelihood

---

4   Though, as we have noted, advanced economies have not always gathered aggregate income data.

that different types of happiness evidence will be deemed more or less acceptable, is an ideal vehicle for policy-based evidence, rather than evidence-based policy. It does not seem that its widespread use would be conducive to good governance.

We suggest instead that good governance relies on efficiency of information; the use of those measures and metrics which are the most accurate and reliable, least prone to distortion through incentive incompatibility and biased interpretation, the independent trends in which are identifiable, and which can be expected to change at least partially predictably in response to relevant decisions. Metrics that do not have these properties give decision-makers little means of knowing whether they have made the wrong or the right decisions. A wise politician understands that the chain of reasoning is as strong as its weakest informational link, admits to what he cannot know and devolves responsibility accordingly. He has confidence that those he governs are capable of taking on responsibility, and he understands that it can be a source of contentment and self-respect in itself. He does not seek to accrue so much responsibility that he needs to constantly expand the set of things he controls and measures.

Until relatively recently, many well-meaning people on the left believed that the state should play an active role in the day-to-day running of industry. Following the abject failure of central planning in the Soviet bloc, there are few takers for this position today. But the reflex to reductively pinpoint capitalism as the root of all evil, the urge to intervene, the belief that the expert knows better than the ordinary person what is good for him or her, are incurable. Happiness research is one of the latest manifestations of this tendency. But, just like central planning, it is inherently flawed.

Appendix 1
CHANGES IN THE HAPPINESS INDEX

The implications for the number of individuals moving between different happiness categories of any given change in the Happiness Index are set out below. For simplicity, the three-point scale of happiness is used, though the approach can readily be generalised to n point scales.

Happiness Index H is calculated as follows as the average of self-expressed happiness:

$$H = \frac{N_1 + 2N_2 + 3N_3}{N_1 + N_2 + N_3} = n_1 + 2n_2 + 3n_3 \qquad (1)$$

Where N_i is the absolute number of people in happiness category i (1 = not very happy, 2 = fairly happy, 3 = very happy), and n_i is the proportion in category i.

As $n_1 + n_2 + n_3 = 1$, one of the n_i can be substituted into (1):

$$H = 1 - n_2 - n_3 + 2n_2 + 3n_3 = 1 + n_2 + 2n_3 \qquad (2)$$

A change in H from an original level H° is expressed as follows:

$$H^\circ + \Delta H = 1 + n_2^\circ + 2n_3^\circ + \Delta n_{12} - \Delta n_{23} + 2\Delta n_{23} + 2\Delta n_{13}$$
$$\Delta H = \Delta n_{12} + \Delta n_{23} + 2\Delta n_{13} \qquad (3)$$

where Δn_{ij} is the net proportion of people going from category i to category j.

Therefore, for a change in H of 0.01, you would have to get 1 per cent of people going up one category, or 0.5 per cent of people going up two categories, or some combination of the two.

Appendix 2
STATISTICAL APPENDIX

In this appendix, we document some straightforward statistical analysis of mean US happiness over the period 1971–2003. The data on happiness is taken from the World Database of Happiness at www1.eur.nl/fsw/happiness/. The specific happiness data has the code O-HL/c/sq/v/3/aa in this database, and is the mean value of the responses to the question:

'Taken all together, how would you say things are these days? Would you say that you are …

3 very happy?
2 pretty happy?
1 not too happy?'

For a number of the earlier years, the data is available for several different months of the year. In these cases, the average of the readings is taken to be the data for the year as a whole. Data is available for each year from 1971 to 1991 except 1979 and 1981. It is also available for 1993 and 1994, and from then on biannually until 2004.

The minimum value recorded is 2.15 and the maximum 2.25. It is worth noting, however, that the value did fluctuate markedly during the course of a single year. For example, in 1973 the value reported for different months varied between 2.11 and 2.23, and in

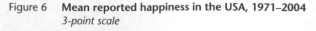

Figure 6   **Mean reported happiness in the USA, 1971–2004**
3-point scale

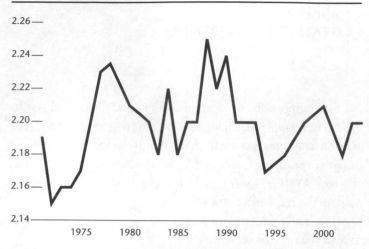

Note: data available 1971–78, 1980, 1982–92, 1993, 1994, 1996, 1998, 2000, 2002 and 2004.

1974 there was even greater variation. The mean value for February of that year was 2.03 and for March 2.25. The fact that variations during the course of a single year appear to be just as large as variations in individual years measured across decades does suggest that changes in the data may not be related to systematic trends in society and the economy.

The relatively low values in the early 1970s may give the impression that mean happiness has risen gradually over time. A simple regression of happiness against a time variable (1971 = 1) does give a positive coefficient on time, but not one that is significantly different from zero.

Almost all the analysis of happiness and macro-level variables focuses on the lack of correlation between real GDP per head and happiness. This is readily confirmed. The source for real US GDP per head at 2000 prices is Johnston and Williamson (2006). The simple correlation between the two variables is only 0.225. At the conventional level of statistical significance (5 per cent) with this number of observations, the correlation needs to be over 0.33 to be judged significantly different from zero, and even at the 10 per cent level it needs to be over 0.26 (assuming that we expect the relationship between the two to be positive).

We also analysed the correlation between mean annual happiness and the following variables:

- the Gini coefficient of income inequality;
- the violent crime rate per 100,000 population;
- the property crime rate per 100,000 population;
- the unemployment rate;
- life expectancy;
- inequality between male and female earnings.

The Gini coefficient is calculated by the US Census Bureau (www.census.gov/hhes/www/income/income.html). The Census Bureau is also the source for life expectancy (*National Vital Statistics Reports*, 54(14), 19 April 2006, Table 12. Estimated life expectancy at birth in years, by race and sex: Death-registration States, 1900–28, and United States, 1929–2003). The crime rates are provided by the Bureau of Justice (www.ojp.usdoj.gov/bjs/). The Bureau of Labor Statistics gives the unemployment rate (www.bls.gov/cps/prev_yrs.htm) and the ratio of median female to male earnings of full-time workers aged over fifteen (Table P-40. Women's Earnings as a Percentage of Men's Earnings by Race and

Figure 7   Mean US happiness and Gini coefficient, 1971–2004

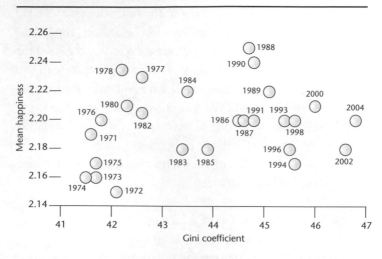

Hispanic Origin: 1960 to 2003): this latter variable is taken as a proxy for inequality between the sexes.

Figures 7 to 12 respectively plot the mean happiness data against the Gini coefficient, the violent crime rate, the property crime rate, the unemployment rate, life expectancy and inequality between the sexes. The data for inequality between the sexes and for life expectancy are only available to 2003.

The simple correlation coefficient between the happiness measure and the Gini coefficient is 0.22, well below the conventional level of statistical significance.[1] Inspection of the chart reveals clearly that different levels of happiness are recorded at

---

1   The null hypothesis that each of these variables follows a normal distribution is not violated dramatically in any individual case, and so conventional t-tests are valid in this context.

Figure 8   Mean US happiness and violent crime rate, 1971–2004

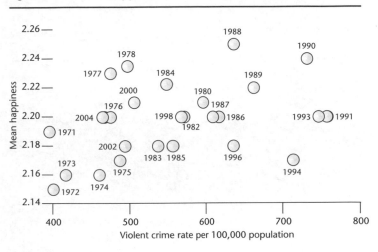

very similar levels of income inequality.

Figure 8 suggests that there is a *positive* relationship between happiness and the violent crime rate. The correlation is in fact 0.374, indicating that it is statistically significantly different from zero.

Figure 9 below gives the impression again of a positive correlation between happiness and property crime. In this case, the formal correlation is 0.484, definitely significantly different from zero.

In Figures 10 and 11 overleaf, the correlation between happiness and the unemployment rate is just –0.05, not at all significantly different from zero, and between happiness and life expectancy it is only 0.167, again not significantly different from zero.

Figure 9   **Mean US happiness and property crime rate, 1971–2004**

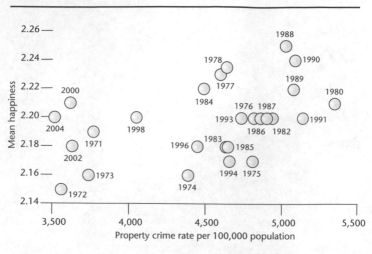

So in terms of the simple correlation with happiness, there is definitely no correlation with real GDP per head, income inequality, unemployment, or equality between male and female earnings. There is a positive correlation with life expectancy. But there is also a positive correlation with both the violent crime rate and property crime rates (these two variables are by no means completely correlated with each other over time, their correlation being 0.62).

There are statistical issues concerning how appropriate it is to correlate the raw data for happiness and, say, life expectancy. By definition, the happiness data is bounded in the range [1, 3] and so in the long run cannot exhibit any trend. Over any given small sample of data it may do so, but by definition any such trend cannot continue indefinitely, because the happiness rating has an

Figure 10 **Mean US happiness and unemployment rate, 1971–2004**

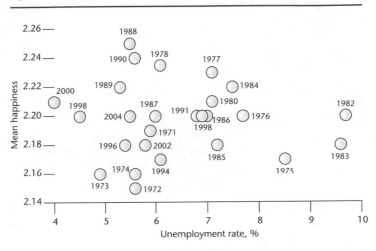

upper bound. In principle, life expectancy is unbounded and so can exhibit a trend not just in a small sample of data but in the long run. The same applies to real GDP per capita. In contrast, and again by definition, the Gini coefficient, the unemployment rate and the female/male earnings ratio are bounded within fixed limits.

We therefore examine the correlations between the happiness data in its basic form (i.e. the level of happiness) and the proportionate change in real GDP per head and life expectancy. Transforming the variables in this way removes the trends observed in the data. The correlation between happiness and GDP transformed in this way is 0.167, again not significantly different from zero. The significance observed in the correlation between happiness and life expectancy in level form is removed when the

Figure 11   **Mean US happiness and life expectancy, 1971–2002**

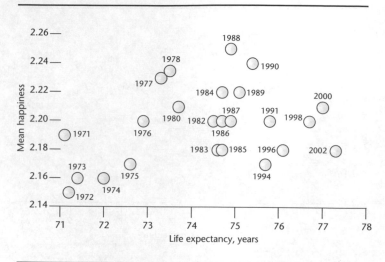

proportionate change in life expectancy is used, the estimated correlation being –0.167.

For completeness, the correlations between happiness in level form and the proportionate changes in the other variables are: Gini coefficient –0.022; violent crime 0.158; property crime –0.151; unemployment –0.250; equality between male and female earnings 0.148. In other words, none of the correlations between happiness and the proportionate change in the other variables is significantly different from zero.

Out of interest, we correlated the proportionate change in happiness with the proportionate change in the other variables. All except two were not significantly different from zero. The correlation with unemployment is –0.386, and with real GDP per head 0.372.

Figure 12 **Mean US happiness and equality between sexes, 1971–2002**

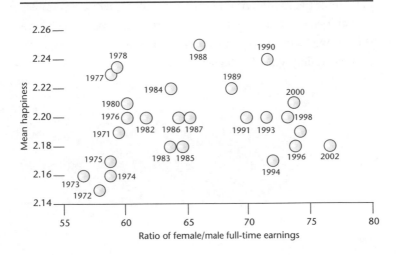

We can go on to examine the effect of these variables on happiness using multiple regression. In other words, by regressing happiness on all of these variables and seeing which ones have a significant impact on happiness, taking into account the impacts of the others. We experimented with various specifications. For example, using all the variables in their original level forms; regressing the level of happiness on the level of all other variables except GDP and life expectancy, which were in proportionate change form; the level of happiness on all variables in proportionate change form; and all variables in proportionate change form. We estimated the general forms, using all explanatory variables, and then eliminated the least significant in sequence.

But however we specify the regression, the results remain wholly unsatisfactory, just as the simple correlation results are.

The significance of a variable is sensitive to the particular specification of the model. And in each regression there are variables whose coefficients are significantly different from zero which have the 'wrong' sign. For example, crime appearing with a positive coefficient, implying that higher crime increases happiness.

REFERENCES

Akerlof, G. A. (1970), 'The market for "lemons": quality
   uncertainty and the market mechanism', *Quarterly Journal of
   Economics*, 84(3): 488–500.
Becker, G. S. (1981), *A Treatise on the Family*, Chicago, IL:
   University of Chicago Press.
Becker, G. and L. Rayo (2006), 'Evolutionary efficiency and mean
   reversion in happiness', Graduate Business School, University
   of Chicago.
Brickman, P., D. Coates and R. Janoff-Bulman (1978), 'Lottery
   winners and accident victims: is happiness relative?', *Journal
   of Personality and Social Psychology*, 36(8): 917–27.
Crafts, N. (2002), *Britain's Relative Economic Performance 1870–
   1999*, London: Institute for Economic Affairs.
Daly, H. and J. Cobb (1989), *For the Common Good*, Boston, MA:
   Beacon Press.
De Botton, A. (2004), *Status Anxiety*, London: Penguin.
Di Tella, R. and R. MacCulloch (2006), 'Some uses of happiness
   data in economics', *Journal of Economic Perspectives*, 20: 25–47.
Di Tella, R., R. J. MacCulloch and A. J. Oswald (2003), 'The
   macroeconomics of happiness', *Review of Economics and
   Statistics*, 85(4): 809–27.

Diener, E. and E. M. Suh (1999), 'National differences in subjective wellbeing', in D. Kahneman, E. Diener and N. Schwarz (eds), *Well Being: The Foundations of Hedonic Psychology*, New York: Russell-Sage.

Dolan, P. and T. Peasgood (2006), 'Valuing non-market goods: does subjective wellbeing offer a viable alternative to contingent valuation?', working paper presented to 'Accounting for the best things in life: wellbeing research and economic valuation', a seminar organised by the UK Network of Environmental Economists, 10 July 2006, available at www.eftec.co.uk/home.php?section=8&uknee=1&seminar=7.

Dolan, P., T. Peasgood, A. Dixon, M. Knight, D. Phillips, A. Tsuchiya and M. White (2006), 'Research on the relationship between wellbeing and sustainable development', final report for the UK Department for Environment, Food and Rural Afairs, available at www.sustainable-development.gov.uk/publications/pdf/WellbeingProject3A.pdf.

Duesenberry, J. S. (1948), 'Income–consumption relations and their implications', in L. Metzler et al., *Income, Employment and Public Policy*, New York: Norton.

Easterlin, R. A. (1974), 'Does economic growth improve the human lot?', in P. A. David and M. W. Reder (eds), *Nations and Households in Economic Growth: Essays in Honor of Moses Abramovitz*, New York: Academic Press.

Easterlin, R. A. (2003), 'Explaining happiness', *Proceedings of the National Academy of Sciences*, 100(19): 11176–83.

Easterlin, R. A. (2005), 'Diminishing marginal utility of income? Caveat emptor', *Social Indicators Research*, 70: 243–55, available at www-rcf.usc.edu/~easterl/articles.html.

Engle, R. F. and C. W. J. Granger (1987), 'Co-integration and error correction: representation, estimation, and testing', *Econometrica*, 55: 251–76.

Frey, B. S. and A. Stutzer (2002a), 'What can economists learn from happiness research?', *Journal of Economic Literature*, XL: 402–35.

Frey, B. S. and A. Stutzer (2002b), *Happiness and Economics*, Princeton, NJ: Princeton University Press.

Hamilton, K. and M. Clemens (1999), 'Genuine savings rates in developing countries', *World Bank Economic Review*, 13: 333–56.

HMT (Her Majesty's Treasury) (2003), *Green Book: Appraisal and Valuation in Central Government*, available on the Treasury website.

Johnston, L. D. and S. H. Williamson (2006), *The Annual Real and Nominal GDP for the United States, 1790–Present*, Economic History Services, 1 April 2006, http://eh.net/hmit/gdp/.

Kahneman, D. (2002), 'Maps of bounded rationality', Nobel Prize lecture, available at www.nobelprize.org/nobel_prizes/economics/laureates/2002/kahneman-lecture.html.

Kahneman, D. (2006), 'The science of wellbeing', Seminar at the Institute for Public Policy Research, London, 1 September 2006.

Kahneman, D. and A. Krueger (2006), 'Developments in the measure of subjective wellbeing', *Journal of Economic Perspectives*, 20: 3–24.

Kuznets, S. (1971), 'Modern economic growth: findings and reflections', Nobel Prize lecture, available at www.nobelprize.org/nobel_prizes/economics/laureates/1971/kuznets-lecture.html.

Laury, J. S. E., G. R. Lewis and P. A. Ormerod (1978), 'Properties of macroeconomic models of the UK: a comparative study', *National Institute Economic Review*, 83(1): 52–72.

Layard, R. (2005), *Happiness: Lessons from a New Science*, London: Allen Lane.

Loh, E. S. (1996), 'Productivity differences and the marriage wage premium for white males', *Journal of Human Resources*, 31: 566–89.

Loomes, G., C. Starmer and R. Sugden (1991), 'Observing violations of transitivity by experimental methods', *Econometrica*, 59: 425–42.

Maurice, R. (1968), *National Accounts: Sources and Methods*, London: HMSO.

NEF (New Economics Foundation) (2004), 'A wellbeing manifesto for a flourishing society', available at the NEF website, www.neweconomics.org/gen/z_sys_ PublicationDetail.aspx?pid=193.

Nordhaus, W. and J. Tobin (1972), *Is Growth Obsolete?*, New York: Columbia University Press.

OECD (Organisation for Economic Cooperation and Development) (2006), OECD Productivity Database, available at www.oecd.org/dataoecd/28/18/36396770.xls.

Ormerod, P. and C. Mounfield (2000), 'Random matrix theory and the failure of macro-economic forecasting', *Physica A*, 280: 497–504.

Oswald, A. J. (2005), 'On the common claim that happiness equations demonstrate diminishing marginal utility of income', University of Warwick Department of Economics paper, available at www.andrewoswald.com.

Oswald, A. J. and N. Powdthavee (2006), 'Does happiness adapt? A longitudinal study of disability with implications for economists and judges', IZA Discussion Paper no. 2208, available at www.ssrn.com/abstract=921040.

Perman, R., Y. Ma, J. McGilvray and M. Common (1999), *Natural Resource and Environmental Economics*, London: Pearson.

SDRN (Sustainable Development Research Network) (2006), *Wellbeing Concepts and Challenges*, SDRN Briefing 3, available at www.sd-research.org.uk/wellbeing/documents/FinalWellbeingPolicyBriefing.pdf.

Smith, V. L. (2002), 'Constructivist and ecological rationality in economics', Nobel Prize lecture, available at www.nobelprize.org/nobel_prizes/economics/laureates/2002/smith-lecture.html.

Van Praag, B. (2004), 'How to find compensations for aircraft noise nuisance', in B. Van Praag and A. Ferrer-I-Carbonell (eds), *Happiness Quantified: A Satisfaction Calculus Approach*, Oxford: Oxford University Press.

Veenhoven, R. (2007), World Database of Happiness Bibliography, available at www.worlddatabaseofhappiness.eur.nl.

Wilkinson, W. (2007), 'In pursuit of happiness research: is it reliable? What does it imply for policy?', Policy Analysis 590, Cato Institute, Washington, DC.

Wilson, C. M. and A. J. Oswald (2005), 'How does marriage affect physiological and psychological health? Evidence for longitudinal studies', Discussion paper, Department of Economics, University of Warwick.

Commentary
A DECEPTIVE EUREKA MOMENT
Samuel Brittan[1]

How small of all that human hearts endure
That part which laws or kings can cause or cure!

SAMUEL JOHNSON

Helen Johns and Paul Ormerod have done a splendid job in exposing the futility of much happiness research and its roots in the perennial desire of some people to manage other people's lives and to pull down the affluent by high marginal tax rates that go well beyond any reasonable revenue needs of government. The authors have undertaken a critical study of the questionnaire studies on which much happiness research is based; and they have given some factual details about the one place – the Himalayan state of Bhutan – where gross national happiness is the official basis for policy, which has led, among other things, to compulsory national dress and the oppression of the ethnically Nepalese minority. In the UK the main manifestation of happiness research in public policy so far has been a series of undergraduate-type essays of the type so loved by the Blair Policy Unit. But do not relax too soon: David Cameron has been talking of 'gross national wellbeing' replacing GDP as a policy goal.

---

1   Samuel Brittan is a columnist on the *Financial Times*. He is an honorary fellow of Jesus College. He was knighted in 1993 for 'services to economic journalism'. His latest book is *Against the Flow* (see www.samuelbrittan.co.uk).

The most useful thing I can add is a very abbreviated intellectual history of the happiness debate. Those wanting to delve further are referred to the recently published study by a father-and-son team of philosopher and economist (Kenny and Kenny, 2006).

Words do not have 'essential' meanings and can be used in different ways. One tradition stemming from Aristotle, if not earlier, will only count a person as truly happy if his contentment arises from high-minded activities such as statesmanship or the pursuit of pure mathematics. This is smuggling in by the back door a particular philosopher's idea of a worthwhile life: an objective best argued directly rather than made true by definition.

There is another tradition stemming from the British utilitarians at the end of the eighteenth century which saw happiness in terms of the subjective wellbeing of individual people. A later exponent was John Stuart Mill, who never wavered in the conviction that happiness was the end of life, but who also believed that those who achieve it 'have their minds fixed on some other object', such as the wellbeing of others or some art or pursuit.[2] The two Kenny authors follow a similar track in their emphasis on the human ability to adapt. People get used to more income, but also to worse health. As much of the cross-country variation in subjective wellbeing remains unexplained by objective influences they suggest that there is 'a distinct limit to policy or other interventions' aimed at increasing subjective wellbeing scores.

For most of the time since then there has been little conflict between the ideals of promoting happiness and maximising individual choice. Jeremy Bentham would have liked a happiness

2   Unfortunately he spoilt his own case by a priggish distinction between 'higher' and 'lower' pleasures.

meter. But in its absence he and those who followed him interpreted happiness in terms of the opportunity to satisfy desires; and the only way they knew of examining these desires operationally was in terms of actual choices as revealed in the market and elsewhere: a doctrine known as revealed preference. 'Choice utilitarianism' is a useful label to demarcate this doctrine from Bentham's original concept.

This shift towards choice was indeed welcome to those of us who put personal freedom and choice above whatever a happiness meter might show. But this has always irked those economists who instinctively prefer collective to individual judgement and who have a deep-seated desire to interfere with marketplace choices.

One should not exaggerate the difference between the choice utilitarians and the advocates of direct happiness measures. They stand together against many other proposed goals of national policy, ranging from the glorification of the state to the triumph of a particular religion or the promotion of some ideology, whether Marxism or fundamentalist Christianity.

There has nevertheless come a parting of the ways between choice utilitarians who are interested in maximising individual opportunities and those more concerned to construct a technocratic Brave New World. Towards the end of the twentieth century some of the economists in the latter camp found a way of making a counter-attack by the simple means of administering questionnaires to people about their wellbeing or satisfaction at various times. Such questionnaire studies have been used for over a century by some of the other social sciences to which economists regard themselves as so superior. Nevertheless, they came as a eureka moment to economists intent on a retreat from individualism.

The issue has been well put by an American philosopher, Neera Bhadwar, in what is by far the most illuminating contribution to an issue of the *Philosopher's Magazine* (third quarter, 2006) devoted to happiness. He discusses the idea of penalising hard workers and high earners who labour for long hours, supposedly to improve their life balance and to reduce the opportunities for envy and jealousy by people lower down the income scale. Bhadwar writes in opposition:

> People are different and find fulfilment and meaning in
> different sorts of worthwhile lives, with different mixes of
> work and pleasure, a mix that they have both the right and
> best qualifications to choose for themselves. And so we
> should have reservations about any one-size-fits-all policy
> designed to push people into more downtime [leisure time]
> (even assuming the policy would have this effect and not the
> contrary one of pushing the target group into more work to
> make up for lost income).

He refers to the triumph of the founders of Google, which would not have been possible if Layard's recommendations to make people happier by preventing them from working too long and earning too much had been implemented by the US government.

The 'happiness' advocates make a great debating point by assuming that those who do not follow them are committed to maximising GDP. While this may be true of *lumpeneconomists* who pontificate on the latest indicators, it is certainly untrue of mainstream economists whose textbooks are full of warnings about the inadequacies of GDP as a welfare indicator for a variety of reasons ranging from the omission of 'bads' such as pollution to the failure to account for leisure or the contribution made by household work, which does not come within the cash nexus.

In advanced Western countries it is reasonable to expect governments to concentrate on their core functions of internal and external security, providing public goods that the market cannot provide and trying to correct for the worse spillover effects of our activities upon each other. I would also include redistribution towards the less fortunate, which need not depend on envy and resentment. In doing all this, the failures of the commercial marketplace have to be weighed against the failures of the political marketplace on which we have been formally enlightened by American public choice theorists. But surely matters such as obesity, 'respect' and so much else on the Blairite agenda ought to be left to individuals.

Governments are still a long way from successfully carrying out their basic tasks. Meanwhile we should leave preaching about the good life to the archbishops, who may know as much or as little about it as the bright young people who write papers for 10 Downing Street.

Postcript on *Brave New World*

I sometimes advise people interested in the happiness debate to reread Aldous Huxley's novel *Brave New World*, published in 1932. In contrast to Orwell's *Nineteen Eighty-Four*, people are not made to conform by fear of Big Brother. They are conditioned to do so by a selective breeding system, and they readily accept their division into alphas, betas, gammas, deltas and epsilons – the latter of course being those who do all the world's dirty work. But as a precaution there is a drug, soma, to be taken at any sign of waning happiness.

What is wrong with this dystopia? I cannot really use my

freedom argument as the inhabitants have been conditioned not to yearn for something they have never known. Some distasteful features, such as electric shocks given to young children to induce distaste for flowers and books, arise from the way Huxley has constructed his narrative and are not an essential feature. To my mind the real weak spot is soma. Throughout his life Huxley was looking for a real-life equivalent and ended up by recommending mescaline. But to the best of my knowledge there are no happiness drugs devoid of unfortunate side- and after-effects and which would allow the work of the world to continue if universally taken. Nor are there likely to be. If there were a genuine soma I would have to rethink my attitudes, as would most other people.

References

Kenny, A. and C. Kenny (2006), *Life, Liberty and the Pursuit of Utility: Happiness in Philosophical and Economic Thought*, St. Andrew's Studies in Philosophy and Public Affairs, Imprint Academic.

Commentary
HAPPINESS, RATIONALITY AND WELFARE
Melanie Powell[1]

In general, I share many of the concerns raised by Helen Johns and Paul Ormerod about the potential for using happiness measures for the development of economic policy. In particular, I agree that there are serious methodological problems in studies using limited-value measures of happiness and that the problems of accurate prediction and control of macroeconomic variables are likely to apply to happiness. I am not, however, convinced by the conclusion that happiness data is an insensitive measure of welfare. It is still possible that aggregate social welfare has not varied substantially over time.

Even supposing that happiness could be measured on a continuous scale and used as a proxy for utility, the current evidence from behavioural economics and psychology suggests that the human mind is not designed for maximisation of welfare or happiness (see reviews by Kahneman and Krueger, 2006, and Frey and Stutzer, 2002). Rather, the human mind is designed to recognise patterns and follow processes that lead to repeated errors which contradict rationality. Current evidence suggests that the economic policy model for maximising money values is flawed (Read and Powell, 2002). The axiomatic revealed-preference theory, where rational economic agents make choices from

---

1   Melanie Powell is Principal Lecturer in the Department of Business, Computing and Law at the University of Derby.

which utility can be inferred, is becoming increasingly untenable (McFadden, 1999). Economists must look more closely at inter-personal comparisons of welfare, where welfare is influenced by consistent biases in behaviour.

We cannot get away from the policy problem of maximising social welfare. A benign rational social welfare maximising authority can supposedly raise aggregate social welfare by second- or third-best actions evaluated by a cost–benefit analysis. If we cannot rely on positivist theory to maximise welfare or happiness, then we must turn to normative theory. Can and should governments use economic incentives to alter people's behaviour to raise social welfare or happiness? Is there any representative political system whereby this can be achieved without sacrificing individual welfare? We have not solved the 'impossibility' problem of aggregating the social welfare function through policy in economics, and a better measure of happiness will not resolve this. In addition, improvements in happiness appear to decay over time. Economic policy would need to weigh current happiness against future happiness, as well as determine the distribution of happiness between individuals and groups. It is reasonable to think that the redistribution of happiness would suffer from the same 'leaky bucket' problems of efficiency loss as the redistribution of income.

The research on happiness has, however, raised useful policy issues. For example, the positive link between happiness and the extent of representative government is interesting (Frey and Stutzer, 2002). If welfare is affected by subjective feelings of perceived control, then the efficiency of government policy may be increased by small changes in local control, local trust, referenda and transparency. If aspiration and adaptation, and *ex post* evaluation of rising income, limit increases in perceived welfare, then policy may need to provide the public with stronger and more salient reference points for judging welfare changes (Read and Powell, 2002).

It appears that both traditional positivist economic theory and the growth of subjective wellbeing theory have a long way to go. While the existing focus of much economic policy on GNP growth may be theoretically flawed, the authors are right to argue that a switch to a focus on happiness is unjustified.

References

Frey, B. S. and A. Stutzer (2002), 'What can economists learn from happiness research?', *Journal of Economic Literature*, XL: 402–35.

Kahneman, D. and A. Krueger (2006), 'Developments in the measure of subjective wellbeing', *Journal of Economic Perspectives*, 20: 3–24.

McFadden, D, (1999), 'Rationality for economists', *Journal of Risk and Uncertainty*, 19(1–3): 73–105.

Read, D. and M. Powell (2002), 'Reasons for sequence preferences over time', *Journal of Behavioural Decision Making*, 15(5): 433–60.

A REJOINDER
Helen Johns and Paul Ormerod

In our rejoinder, we do not wish to comment on Samuel Brittan's commentary, though we thank him for making some excellent and very interesting points. Clearly there is a large measure of agreement between us. Melanie Powell has raised some interesting issues that we would like to comment on here and which should be the subject of wider debate. They are not necessarily disagreements with the basic thrust of the monograph but there is a difference of emphasis which we would like to discuss further. We also discuss some comments that Richard Layard has made about a journal article we have written in anticipation of the publication of this monograph.

Powell makes a number of points about how the axiomatic model of rationality in economics is not in general supported by the empirical evidence. We are very sympathetic to this view, and have stated this extensively in print, including in Chapter 2 of this monograph, which concludes 'happiness research is a useful part of the modern research programme in economics. Its findings fit in with the wide range of evidence in the more general field of experimental and behavioural economics. In general, economics needs different postulates on individual behaviour to the conventional one of utility maximisation.'

Further, we have successfully addressed empirical questions with theoretical models in which agent behaviour is very decidedly non-rational. An early example of this is the paper by Paul Ormerod and Helen Johns: 'System fitness and the extinction of firms under pure economic competition', Paper of the Month on the World Econophysics website (www.unifr.ch/econophysics/), August 2001. More recent examples are Ormerod (2006a, 2006b) and Ormerod and Colbaugh (2006). The issue of rationality was not, however, one we intended to cover in any detail in the monograph, and readers should certainly not take it as a defence of one side in a polarised debate about 'happiness versus rational economic man'.

In fact this dichotomy is of minor relevance to the monograph – it is not mentioned in our bullet list of 'principal criticisms' on page 21, for example. Rather, the monograph is about whether happiness evidence can be relied upon to give an objective, cross-verifiable and internally consistent measure of real social processes which can be used to make better policy decisions at a national level. If policy indicators cannot be causally linked to either other socio-economic indicators or past policy decisions, then what do they really bring to the policymaker's toolbox?

Melanie Powell states that she is not convinced by the conclusion that happiness data is an insensitive measure of welfare, and that it is still possible that aggregate social welfare has not varied substantially over time. She offers no evidence for this latter view, so it is not possible to respond to it directly. We maintain, however, that happiness data is a grossly insensitive measure of welfare – not because we 'know' that overall happiness has increased over the time periods discussed (which we concede we do not), but for the following reason. Happiness is measured in discrete steps, with a fairly large qualitative difference between these steps, with the result that the measurement is incapable of picking up on small, incremental changes that make people's lives better, particularly as people are likely to become habituated to small, incremental changes.

Further, as described at length in the monograph, changes in the Happiness Index cannot be linked to other processes that most reasonable people would imagine to have made real improvements to people's welfare. And if the Happiness Index does not even decrease in parallel with a claimed large rise in reported depression, then it cannot in any way be claimed to be sensitive to what it is supposed to be measuring. Instead, the small movements observed in it seem to be somewhat (but perhaps not entirely) random fluctuations. In fact, if you look at the raw data in the World Database of Happiness, in some cases data points within years seem to fluctuate as much as data points between years.

The final point to note is that Powell states that 'We cannot get away from the policy problem of maximising social welfare'. Given that she does not believe – quite rightly – that individual agents are capable of following maximising precepts of behaviour, the idea that remote policy makers with no knowledge of others' individual circumstances are able to do so in their stead should be treated with a great deal of scepticism.

In this rejoinder, we would also like to take the opportunity to make some comment on an article by Richard Layard in the June edition of the journal *Prospect* (entitled 'Against Unhappiness'). Professor Layard's article was itself a comment on our summary article based on the ideas in this monograph in the April edition of *Prospect*, entitled 'Against Happiness'. Professor Layard was invited to write a commentary in this monograph, but was unable to take up the opportunity.

Richard Layard has criticised us for not offering a constructive alternative to basing government policy on measured happiness. We should have been more explicit – our alternative is democracy and good governance. Layard asks by what criterion we should chart our course through conflicting societal goals such as liberty, equality and prosperity if not happiness. But to imagine that there is a definitive 'correct' answer to this, rather than a need for constant democratic renegotiation, is somewhat missing the point of democracy. Furthermore, the idea that a measured happiness criterion can transcend conflict between several desirable goals is wholly incorrect.

Layard states that we criticise advocates of the use of measured happiness as a policy guide for concluding from the lack of correlation between measured happiness and variables such as income, public spending, leisure and so on that these variables do not affect happiness. This is not, in fact, our criticism. We criticise the simplistic explanation that happiness measures are static because government is seeking to maximise narrowly defined measures of economic welfare rather than trying to maximise happiness. We are not party to ministerial decisions, but a glance at Cabinet Office or Treasury policy appraisal guidance, not to mention the many indicators listed in Public Service Agreements, would demonstrate that this claim is a hugely misleading oversimplification. Why would government pay for the health treatment of people too old to work if this were true?

If happiness is not increasing, and one believes this to be the ultimate mark of government failure, one might as well argue that it is the sum of democratically determined government policy which has failed, rather than just economic policy. But that, again, would seem rather undemocratic. Alternatively, if no trends in measured happiness are observed despite dramatic changes in society, then perhaps happiness measures are simply a very poor and insensitive measure of welfare. If this is so, then using happiness measures as the ultimate yardstick for policy is a very bad idea; in fact the only purpose such measures would serve would be to create another rod for the government's back when it 'fails' to increase what is clearly an inherently sluggish indicator.

Layard explains that the flatness in the measured happiness trend arises because the positive effects of economic growth have been offset by a deterioration in the quality of our relationships. This is a completely different explanation from the one expounded at length in his book, *Happiness: Lessons from a New Science*, which is that we do not get happier with increased income because of the persistence of income inequality. It is possible that one explanation has seamlessly supplanted the other because neither can be adequately supported by a happiness time series so devoid of information content that it has no explanatory power. This is hardly a promising starting point for a measure on which to base government policy.

In his *Happiness* Layard also claims that people adapt almost entirely to increased income, so it is surprising that happiness gains from income could precisely and consistently offset an upsetting breakdown in human relationships. Note that deterioration in our relationships has not made us unhappier, it has just offset any happiness gained from economic growth. The implication of this logic is that policymakers should be indifferent if our community and family relationships deteriorate as long as we are materially compensated, as we will be just as well off. This is a highly morally dubious result.

Layard dismisses our concerns over 'the dangers of information failure', but these dangers are real. Self-delusion, incompetence and misdirected energies within government, as well as disillusionment, cynicism and mistrust amongst the electorate are the consequences of ignoring these dangers. If government can spin sheer fantasy on supposedly easily enumerable, objective indicators (such as the claim that youth unemployment has been 'virtually abolished' when it is higher than it was in 1997), a preoccupation with people's intimate emotional states would take it straight to cloud cuckoo land.

Layard's claims for this new 'science' of happiness are so strongly reminiscent of 1930s arguments that freedom and prosperity could only be achieved through scientific planning, that quoting Hayek is irresistible. Like economic planning, happiness arguments 'presuppose a much more complete agreement on the relative importance of the different social ends than actually exists', and in order to disguise this, planners replace individual conscience and learned experience with a self-evidently correct moral code (increasing measured happiness). The democratic process is a hindrance to creating the 'right' result, while those with alternative concerns from those of the planners are regarded as simply unreasonable. This is foreshadowed by Layard's comment that we quibble over information failure while 'in the meantime [people] are becoming no happier'. How remiss.

A well-functioning democracy, economic freedom and a government with a grip on reality are admittedly modest aims compared with the maximisation of world happiness, but they nevertheless require a certain effort to maintain. We are hardly likely to advance these aims by upholding a single over-arching societal goal with which all right-thinking opinion should concur. When such a proposal starts to find a foothold of influence – and particularly when it raises serious intellectual question marks – its proposers should anticipate the critical scrutiny which is in the public interest.

References

Ormerod, P. (2006a), 'Economic modelling with low cognition agents', *Physica A*, 307.

Ormerod, P. (2006b), 'Extracting deep knowledge from limited information', *Proceedings of the US Office of Naval Research conference*, Budapest.

Ormerod, P. and R. Colbaugh (2006), 'Cascades of failure and extinction in evolving complex systems', *Journal of Artificial Societies and Social Simulation*, 4.

ABOUT THE IEA

The Institute is a research and educational charity (No. CC 235 351), limited by guarantee. Its mission is to improve understanding of the fundamental institutions of a free society by analysing and expounding the role of markets in solving economic and social problems.

The IEA achieves its mission by:

- a high-quality publishing programme
- conferences, seminars, lectures and other events
- outreach to school and college students
- brokering media introductions and appearances

The IEA, which was established in 1955 by the late Sir Antony Fisher, is an educational charity, not a political organisation. It is independent of any political party or group and does not carry on activities intended to affect support for any political party or candidate in any election or referendum, or at any other time. It is financed by sales of publications, conference fees and voluntary donations.

In addition to its main series of publications the IEA also publishes a quarterly journal, *Economic Affairs*.

The IEA is aided in its work by a distinguished international Academic Advisory Council and an eminent panel of Honorary Fellows. Together with other academics, they review prospective IEA publications, their comments being passed on anonymously to authors. All IEA papers are therefore subject to the same rigorous independent refereeing process as used by leading academic journals.

IEA publications enjoy widespread classroom use and course adoptions in schools and universities. They are also sold throughout the world and often translated/reprinted.

Since 1974 the IEA has helped to create a worldwide network of 100 similar institutions in over 70 countries. They are all independent but share the IEA's mission.

Views expressed in the IEA's publications are those of the authors, not those of the Institute (which has no corporate view), its Managing Trustees, Academic Advisory Council members or senior staff.

Members of the Institute's Academic Advisory Council, Honorary Fellows, Trustees and Staff are listed on the following page.

The Institute gratefully acknowledges financial support for its publications programme and other work from a generous benefaction by the late Alec and Beryl Warren.

109

Other papers recently published by the IEA include:

WHO, What and Why?
Transnational Government, Legitimacy and the World Health Organization
Roger Scruton
Occasional Paper 113; ISBN 0 255 36487 3; £8.00

The World Turned Rightside Up
A New Trading Agenda for the Age of Globalisation
John C. Hulsman
Occasional Paper 114; ISBN 0 255 36495 4; £8.00

The Representation of Business in English Literature
Introduced and edited by Arthur Pollard
Readings 53; ISBN 0 255 36491 1; £12.00

Anti-Liberalism 2000
The Rise of New Millennium Collectivism
David Henderson
Occasional Paper 115; ISBN 0 255 36497 0; £7.50

Capitalism, Morality and Markets
Brian Griffiths, Robert A. Sirico, Norman Barry & Frank Field
Readings 54; ISBN 0 255 36496 2; £7.50

A Conversation with Harris and Seldon
Ralph Harris & Arthur Seldon
Occasional Paper 116; ISBN 0 255 36498 9; £7.50

Malaria and the DDT Story
Richard Tren & Roger Bate
Occasional Paper 117; ISBN 0 255 36499 7; £10.00

A Plea to Economists Who Favour Liberty: Assist the Everyman
Daniel B. Klein
Occasional Paper 118; ISBN 0 255 36501 2; £10.00

The Changing Fortunes of Economic Liberalism
Yesterday, Today and Tomorrow
David Henderson
Occasional Paper 105 (new edition); ISBN 0 255 36520 9; £12.50

The Global Education Industry
Lessons from Private Education in Developing Countries
James Tooley
Hobart Paper 141 (new edition); ISBN 0 255 36503 9; £12.50

Saving Our Streams
The Role of the Anglers' Conservation Association in
Protecting English and Welsh Rivers
Roger Bate
Research Monograph 53; ISBN 0 255 36494 6; £10.00

Better Off Out?
The Benefits or Costs of EU Membership
Brian Hindley & Martin Howe
Occasional Paper 99 (new edition); ISBN 0 255 36502 0; £10.00

Buckingham at 25
Freeing the Universities from State Control
Edited by James Tooley
Readings 55; ISBN 0 255 36512 8; £15.00

Lectures on Regulatory and Competition Policy
Irwin M. Stelzer
Occasional Paper 120; ISBN 0 255 36511 X; £12.50

Misguided Virtue
False Notions of Corporate Social Responsibility
David Henderson
Hobart Paper 142; ISBN 0 255 36510 1; £12.50

Should We Have Faith in Central Banks?
Otmar Issing
Occasional Paper 125; ISBN 0 255 36528 4; £7.50

The Dilemma of Democracy
Arthur Seldon
Hobart Paper 136 (reissue); ISBN 0 255 36536 5; £10.00

Capital Controls: a 'Cure' Worse Than the Problem?
Forrest Capie
Research Monograph 56; ISBN 0 255 36506 3; £10.00

The Poverty of 'Development Economics'
Deepak Lal
Hobart Paper 144 (reissue); ISBN 0 255 36519 5; £15.00

Should Britain Join the Euro?
The Chancellor's Five Tests Examined
Patrick Minford
Occasional Paper 126; ISBN 0 255 36527 6; £7.50

Post-Communist Transition: Some Lessons
Leszek Balcerowicz
Occasional Paper 127; ISBN 0 255 36533 0; £7.50

A Tribute to Peter Bauer
John Blundell et al.
Occasional Paper 128; ISBN 0 255 36531 4; £10.00

Employment Tribunals
Their Growth and the Case for Radical Reform
J. R. Shackleton
Hobart Paper 145; ISBN 0 255 36515 2; £10.00

Fifty Economic Fallacies Exposed
Geoffrey E. Wood
Occasional Paper 129; ISBN 0 255 36518 7; £12.50

A Market in Airport Slots
Keith Boyfield (editor), David Starkie, Tom Bass & Barry Humphreys
Readings 56; ISBN 0 255 36505 5; £10.00

Money, Inflation and the Constitutional Position of the Central Bank
Milton Friedman & Charles A. E. Goodhart
Readings 57; ISBN 0 255 36538 1; £10.00

railway.com
Parallels between the Early British Railways and the ICT Revolution
Robert C. B. Miller
Research Monograph 57; ISBN 0 255 36534 9; £12.50

The Regulation of Financial Markets
Edited by Philip Booth & David Currie
Readings 58; ISBN 0 255 36551 9; £12.50

Climate Alarmism Reconsidered
Robert L. Bradley Jr
Hobart Paper 146; ISBN 0 255 36541 1; £12.50

Government Failure: E. G. West on Education
Edited by James Tooley & James Stanfield
Occasional Paper 130; ISBN 0 255 36552 7; £12.50

Corporate Governance: Accountability in the Marketplace
Elaine Sternberg
Second edition
Hobart Paper 147; ISBN 0 255 36542 x; £12.50

The Land Use Planning System
Evaluating Options for Reform
John Corkindale
Hobart Paper 148; ISBN 0 255 36550 0; £10.00

Towards a Liberal Utopia?
Edited by Philip Booth
Hobart Paperback 32; ISBN 0 255 36563 2; £15.00

The Way Out of the Pensions Quagmire
Philip Booth & Deborah Cooper
Research Monograph 60; ISBN 0 255 36517 9; £12.50

Black Wednesday
A Re-examination of Britain's Experience in the Exchange Rate Mechanism
Alan Budd
Occasional Paper 135; ISBN 0 255 36566 7; £7.50

Crime: Economic Incentives and Social Networks
Paul Ormerod
Hobart Paper 151; ISBN 0 255 36554 3; £10.00

The Road to Serfdom *with* **The Intellectuals and Socialism**
Friedrich A. Hayek
Occasional Paper 136; ISBN 0 255 36576 4; £10.00

Money and Asset Prices in Boom and Bust
Tim Congdon
Hobart Paper 152; ISBN 0 255 36570 5; £10.00

The Dangers of Bus Re-regulation
and Other Perspectives on Markets in Transport
John Hibbs et al.
Occasional Paper 137; ISBN 0 255 36572 1; £10.00

The New Rural Economy
Change, Dynamism and Government Policy
Berkeley Hill et al.
Occasional Paper 138; ISBN 0 255 36546 2; £15.00

The Benefits of Tax Competition
Richard Teather
Hobart Paper 153; ISBN 0 255 36569 1; £12.50

Wheels of Fortune
Self-funding Infrastructure and the Free Market Case for a Land Tax
Fred Harrison
Hobart Paper 154; ISBN 0 255 36589 6; £12.50

Were 364 Economists All Wrong?
Edited by Philip Booth
Readings 60; ISBN 978 0 255 36588 8; £10.00

Europe After the 'No' Votes
Mapping a New Economic Path
Patrick A. Messerlin
Occasional Paper 139; ISBN 978 0 255 36580 2; £10.00

The Railways, the Market and the Government
John Hibbs et al.
Readings 61; ISBN 978 0 255 36567 3; £12.50

Corruption: The World's Big C
Cases, Causes, Consequences, Cures
Ian Senior
Research Monograph 61; ISBN 978 0 255 36571 0; £12.50

Choice and the End of Social Housing
Peter King
Hobart Paper 155; ISBN 978 0 255 36568 0; £10.00

Sir Humphrey's Legacy
Facing Up to the Cost of Public Sector Pensions
Neil Record
Hobart Paper 156; ISBN 978 0 255 36578 9; £10.00

The Economics of Law
Cento Veljanovski
Second edition
Hobart Paper 157; ISBN 978 0 255 36561 1; £12.50

Living with Leviathan
Public Spending, Taxes and Economic Performance
David B. Smith
Hobart Paper 158; ISBN 978 0 255 36579 6; £12.50

The Vote Motive
Gordon Tullock
New edition
Hobart Paperback 33; ISBN 978 0 255 36577 2; £10.00

Waging the War of Ideas
John Blundell
Third edition
Occasional Paper 131; ISBN 978 0 255 36606 9; £12.50

The War Between the State and the Family
How Government Divides and Impoverishes
Patricia Morgan
Hobart Paper 159; ISBN 978 0 255 36596 3; £10.00

Capitalism – A Condensed Version
Arthur Seldon
Occasional Paper 140; ISBN 978 0 255 36598 7; £7.50

Catholic Social Teaching and the Market Economy
Philip Booth
Hobart Paperback 34; ISBN 978 0 255 36581 9; £15.00

Adam Smith – A Primer
Eamonn Butler
Occasional Paper 141; ISBN 978 0 255 36608 3; £7.50

All the listed IEA papers, including those that are out of print, can be downloaded from www.iea.org.uk. Purchases can also be made through the website. To order copies of currently available IEA papers, or to enquire about availability, please contact:

Gazelle
IEA orders
FREEPOST RLYS-EAHU-YSCZ
White Cross Mills
Hightown
Lancaster LA1 4XS

Tel: 01524 68765
Fax: 01524 63232
Email: sales@gazellebooks.co.uk

The IEA also offers a subscription service to its publications. For a single annual payment, currently £42.00 in the UK, you will receive every monograph the IEA publishes during the course of a year and discounts on our extensive back catalogue. For more information, please contact:

Adam Myers
Subscriptions
The Institute of Economic Affairs
2 Lord North Street
London SW1P 3LB

Tel: 020 7799 8920
Fax: 020 7799 2137
Website: www.iea.org.uk